Electronic Projects 3

Audio Circuits and Projects

Electronic Projects 3
Audio Circuits and Projects

Graham Bishop

First published 1980 by
THE MACMILLAN PRESS LTD
London and Basingstoke
Associated companies in Delhi Dublin
Hong Kong Johannesburg Lagos Melbourne
New York Singapore and Tokyo

Typeset in 10/11 Univers by
Styleset Limited, Salisbury, Wilts.
and printed in Great Britain by A. Wheaton & Co. Ltd., Exeter

British Library Cataloguing in Publication Data

Bishop, Graham Dudley
   Audio circuits and projects.
   — (Electronic projects; 3).
   1. Sound — Recording and reproducing
   — Amateurs' manuals
   2. Amplifiers, Audio — Amateurs' manuals
   3. Electronic apparatus and appliances —
   Amateurs' manuals 4. Sound — Apparatus
   I. Title II. Series
   621.389'3   TK9968

   ISBN 0—333—27513—6

Contents

Preface

This book is one of a series of electronics hobbies books for electronics constructors at all levels. Almost 100 circuits are described with constructional details given where necessary. The circuits range from those with no integrated circuits or transistors to those with over 15 ICs; all are within the capabilities of the beginner to electronics building.

The first two chapters include some theoretical introduction to the world of audio electronics, where the definitions and jargon are explained. Many hints on construction techniques are also given and the reader is well advised to read these two chapters before plunging into the circuits in the rest of the book. Hints on the purchase of hi-fi equipment and components are included. The circuits of chapters 3 to 7 can be considered as individual modules which can be interlinked to form more complex circuits if desired. A preamplifier and three filters from chapter 3, a power amplifier from chapter 4, a phasing circuit and automatic fade circuit from chapter 5, a sound-to-light unit from chapter 6 and a power supply from chapter 4 together produce a fully comprehensive disco unit with far more facilities than many commercial models.

Neatness of construction and observance of safety precautions are essential. Long wires and shoddy workmanship lead to poor performance, impossible fault-finding and a dangerous piece of equipment, particularly if mains voltages are involved. Constructors need very few tools — a good pair of miniature cutters and pliers with a set of various sized screwdrivers are essential. A 15 or 25 W soldering iron with small bit is required and a simple multimeter for the normal ac/dc ranges are all that are necessary. A signal generator and oscilloscope are useful but not essential — these can often be borrowed.

Components come in all sizes and prices. Bulk packs of resistors, capacitors, transistors, diodes and other components are usually a bargain. Some packs are untested but are quite adequate for the circuits in this book. A diode is tested with an ohmmeter reading about 1k in one direction and several 100k in the other direction. A transistor is tested in the same way, treating the base—emitter and base—collector terminals as two diodes.

Electronics construction is an enjoyable hobby and it should always remain so. It will not be frustrating and expensive if the simple instructions are followed. I hope that you will get much enjoyment out of reading this book and carrying out the circuit-building and testing.

G. D. BISHOP

Publisher's Note

While every effort has been made to ensure the accuracy of the projects and circuits in this book, neither the Publishers nor the author accept liability for any injury or loss resulting from the construction of any of the designs published herein.

The Publishers will, however, be pleased to hear from readers who have corrections to the text or genuine queries, and will refer any such queries to the author.

1
Why Amplifiers?

You may remember seeing old 'His Master's Voice' record labels with a dog listening to the sounds emerging from the horn of an early phonograph. In those days there were no valves or transistors, so manufacturers had to rely on mechanical 'amplification'. The gramophone could produce sounds which, although limited in quality, could fill a medium-sized room. The large horn was a form of acoustic impedance-matching device, its shape being carefully designed (like many brass musical instruments) to throw the maximum amount of sound outwards. Such horns are still used today in horn-speakers for home use and for public-address systems; their output, watt for watt, is far greater than that of the conventional cone type.

The modern electronic amplifier and speaker are far smaller, and can produce louder sounds which are variable both in quality and volume. This chapter describes the required properties of the electronic amplifier so that the amplifier designs of later chapters can reproduce a sound that, to the human ear, is 'hi-fi'.

1.1 The Human Ear

An analysis of the relevant parts of the human ear follows, including frequency response, construction, loudness sensitivity and other aspects which make certain demands on a hi-fi audio system.

1.1.1 Frequency Characteristics

The **audio frequency range** extends from 30 Hz to 20 KHz. The lower limit is difficult to define because, at low frequencies, sound and feeling become difficult to separate. The upper limit is also difficult to define — as we get older, higher frequencies become inaudible. Very loud sounds will damage the ear temporarily or permanently — a three-hour disco session may result in several hours' deafness afterwards.

The central **reference** frequency against which most measurements are made is called the **mid-band frequency** of 1 kHz. The frequency response of figure 1.1 shows the normal plot of amplitude (vertically, measured in decibels) against frequency (horizontally, measured in hertz). The decibel (dB) scale is used because logarithmic scales are shorter and the values can be added and subtracted for a complex system, rather than multiplied and divided on a linear scale. Appendix I gives further details of the mathematics involved in decibel usage.

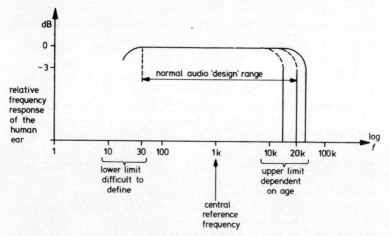

Figure 1.1   The ideal relative frequency response of the human ear

Table 1.1 gives decibel values for various voltage and current ratios, using the mathematics of appendix I.

Some hi-fi amplifiers quote noise and hum figures of 60 dB relative to the signal — known as the **signal-to-noise** dB ratio. This indicates that the signal is one million times stronger than the noise

Table 1.1

dB Value	Voltage Gain $R_{in} = R_{out}$	Current Gain $R_{in} = R_{out}$	Power Gain
100	100 000	100 000	10^{10}
80	10 000	10 000	10^8
60	1000	1000	10^6
40	100	100	10^4
20	10	10	10^2
10	3.2	3.2	10
6	2	2	4.1
3	1.4	1.4	2
0	1	1	1, reference point
−3	1/1.4 = 0.707	1/1.4 = 0.707	1/2, half-power point
−6	1/2	1/2	1/4.1
−10	1/3.2	1/3.2	1/10

or hum at 1 kHz; thus a signal of 1 V has 1 μV of noise superimposed on top — a very small amount, inaudible to the listener (unless he is one of those perfectionists who converts his living room into a multi-million pound recording studio — of which more later). These hi-fi figures also show that, at frequencies lower or higher than 1 kHz, the noise level could be far worse, particularly at 10 kHz and above where it can be more disturbing — statistics can be misleading

The frequency is also plotted on a logarithmic scale, with equal divisions between 1, 10, 1000 and all powers of 10 Hz. Thus a very wide range of frequencies can be shown. Frequency response is often plotted on special **log–log paper**. Hi-fi systems normally concentrate on the **design range**, as shown in figure 1.1, with extension to higher frequencies if necessary (see p. 5).

1.1.2 The Human Ear
The basic components of the ear are shown in figure 1.2: the **pinna**, directed towards the front of the head, the **eardrum** and its three bones which conduct the sound to the sensitive **inner ear**, where the frequency and intensity of the sound are converted into nerve pulses which travel to the brain for processing. The way in which very low and very high frequencies are heard is very complex, the skull playing an active part, along with the eustachian tube that connects the ear to the back of the throat — suffice it to say that the ear works!

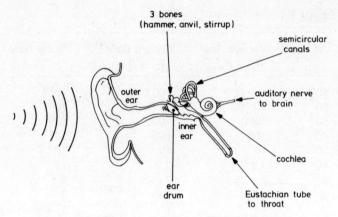

Figure 1.2   Main components of the human ear

Two important points to be made are firstly, that humans have **two** ears, one on the left and one on the right; secondly, the ears are positioned at the main *centre* of communications in the head. These may seem obvious, but the brain can tell the direction of sounds very accurately by decoding the phases and amplitudes of the signals from both ears and distinguishing between different frequencies and sound intensities to either ear. Musicians have a very keen sense of hearing, sometimes as the result of training, and can identify the individual frequencies of a complex mixture of sounds. Try playing a chord on a piano and then whistle or sing the individual notes. Also try closing your eyes and then identifying where a faint sound is coming from in a room — this is relatively simple to do provided neither ear is damaged.

Stereo reproduction uses the ears to give the impression of a 'sound stage' of instruments across about 90°; careful phasing of the left and right signals deceives the ear into this illusion. Mono records are sometimes processed electronically using phasing circuits (see chapter 5) which mislead the ear into thinking that the performers surround the listener. Quadraphony, or surround-sound, represents true 360° using three or four sound sources.

1.1.3 Sound Intensities

Table 1.2 shows the power intensities of sounds (in dB) relative to the **threshold of hearing**. This threshold can only be determined in absolute silence in, say, an anechoic chamber — a room lined with material that will absorb all sounds. Also listed are the sound inten-

Table 1.2 Sound Levels of the Ear

Sound Level (dB)	Intensity (μW/m^2)	Level	Type of Sound
600	10^{14}	Dangerous	Saturn rocket take-off
120	10^6	Very loud	Threshold of pain −
110	10^5		Concorde take-off;
100	10^4		thunder; jet take-off;
90	10^3		Underground train
80	10^2	Loud	Loud motor horn;
70	10		pneumatic drill; heavy
60	1		traffic
50	10^{-1}	Moderate	Ordinary conversation;
40	10^{-2}		inside train or car
30	10^{-3}		
20	10^{-4}	Quiet	Turning page of newspaper;
10	10^{-5}		faint whisper; breathing
0	10^{-6}	Silence	Threshold of hearing

sities (in μW/m^2) of these same sounds, which are related to the dB figures by the mathematical formulae given in appendix I.

Sound levels up to 120 dB give no discomfort, but beyond this level pain and damage to the ear will result. Some amplifiers described later in the book can produce sound levels in excess of 120 dB for amplification in large areas.

1.1.4 High Fidelity
It is most people's ambition to have a true **high fidelity** (hi-fi) system in their home, but what is true hi-fi?

The aim of a hi-fi audio reproduction system is to reproduce perfectly in the home, without any distortion at all, the sounds created in the concert hall or recording studio. However, this aim is unattainable. Figure 1.3a shows the frequency response of the ear, with a defined **bandwidth** between the 3 dB points (also called the **half-power points** − see table 1.1) of 20 kHz. The ear is also able to detect far above 20 kHz, not as direct audio frequencies but as *indirect* audio sounds. Listen to a live concert performance and then to a recording of it − you will notice a distinct loss of quality in the recording. It is difficult to identify what is missing in the recording until you hear a professional recording played back on a system that is sensitive up to 100 kHz − you will immediately sense additional sounds that were missing from the recording up to 15 or 20 kHz.

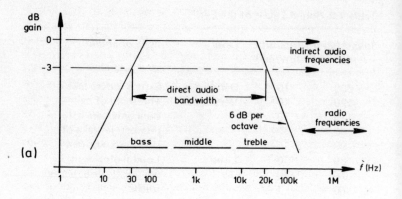

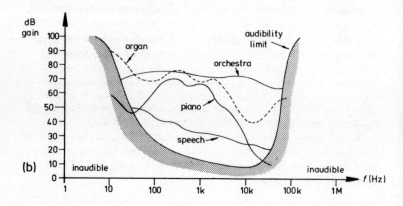

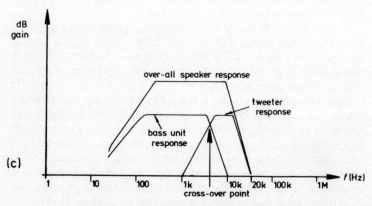

Figure 1.3   Amplifier frequency responses

Unfortunately, an amplifier that is sensitive up to 100 kHz is capable of picking up radio frequencies, which start to appear at 100 kHz (longwave lower limit), so then radio interference becomes a problem. Public-address systems and good hi-fi systems often pick up radio signals, either because they are amplifying 100 kHz signals picked up directly at the amplifier input, or because higher radio frequencies are picked up on the loudspeaker leads — these radio signals travel to the amplifier which detects them and then amplifies them along with the audio signal. Strong taxi transmitters and 'radio ham' transmitters cause much of this interference, and special input filters are needed to filter it out.

The frequency response of the ear is seen to be divided (but not definitively) into **bass, middle** and **treble** ranges. The response also has the normal rise and fall of 6 dB per octave at the lower and upper ends — an **octave** is a frequency of 2 times the **fundamental**, thus 1 kHz has octaves at 2 kHz (the 'second harmonic'), 4 kHz (the 'fourth harmonic'), 8 kHz (the 'eighth harmonic'), and so on. A fall of 6 dB per octave means an attenuation of 6 dB (half gain) from frequency f to frequency $2f$.

Figure 1.3b shows the audible range of the ear relative to the frequency ranges and volumes of speech, a piano, an organ and an orchestra. A hi-fi system should be able to produce all these frequencies and volumes perfectly, otherwise distortion will be heard. This distortion is not necessarily the characteristic distortion heard when an amplifier is overloaded — any deficiency of a waveform, such as added or subtracted frequencies, is regarded as distortion.

The design of electronic circuits which amplify frequencies from 10 Hz to 20 kHz is relatively simple, most modern transistors can amplify frequencies above the audio frequency range. The output is limited mainly by the **loudspeaker**, which converts the high quality electrical audio signal into a mechanical output, or by the input pick-up, which converts the mechanical vibrations of the stylus or diaphragm into electrical signals. Section 1.2 shows why these limitations occur.

One final factor is the *room*. Most living rooms are furnished with carpets, curtains, furniture and people — a variety of sound-absorbent surfaces. Each surface absorbs different frequencies so that the resultant sound heard by the listener bears no relationship to the sound leaving the speaker. The sound also changes as the listener moves about the room, unless a properly designed studio lounge is created with calculated absorbence figures for each surface. True hi-fi cannot therefore be heard in most homes, and for this reason tone controls are incorporated to adjust the amplifier response to suit the surroundings.

1.2 Microphones, Pick-ups and Speakers

The loudspeaker has the worst frequency response of any component in the system. The low frequencies are limited by the construction of the speaker **cone** and the high frequencies by the over-all **damping** of the whole speaker; damping in this case is the inability of the heavy cone to move quickly enough to reproduce the high frequencies. Figure 1.3c shows the simplified response of a bass unit with low response at 10 kHz. Most speaker units compromise with a single unit, in low-priced record players, a double unit (as shown), in medium-fi audio systems, or a treble unit, in hi-fi audio equipment. The contradictory requirements of the bass and treble frequencies can be satisfied in a multi-speaker system, where each speaker is fed with its appropriate range of frequencies from a **cross-over unit** (see chapter 4). The over-all output is the sum of the individual speaker responses, as shown — the low frequency unit is called the **woofer** and the high frequency unit is called the **tweeter**.

The bass unit requires the speaker cone to move relatively slowly over several millimetres or centimetres, while the treble unit requires the cone to move very fast indeed; medium-range units compromise between the two. The speaker shown in figure 1.4e is an electro-mechanical device with an input current fed to the speech coil which is supported between the poles of a very strong magnet. A combination of current and magnetic field causes the coil to move in and out, the coil being physically connected to the speaker cone so that the sound is transmitted outwards. The cone is made of light-weight paper or plastics and is supported flexibly round its edge.

Speaker enclosures are not 'electronic' so they are not described in great detail here, but it must be mentioned that a power amplifier can deliver several amperes of current to the loudspeaker. The speaker speech coil should be designed to carry this current, other-wise smoke output will be substituted for sound output! Always choose a speaker with a **power rating** to match the amplifier and whose **impedance** also matches the amplifier for **maximum power transfer**. Loudspeakers with a **lower** impedance than the amplifier should never be used; speakers with a *higher* impedance can safely be used but the output power will be lower. Series and parallel combinations of speakers can also be used provided the over-all equivalent resistance matches that of the amplifier. A 100 W 8 Ω amplifier, for instance, can drive *four* 25 W 2 Ω speakers connected in series, the sound power being distributed between the individual units, thereby allowing low power speakers to be used rather than the expensive 100 W types.

Many manufacturers quote output power in different forms, using r.m.s. power, music power, peak power, and so on, to advertise the system's amplifier. These figures are often misquoted and may deceive the buyer into thinking that the amplifier is more powerful than it really is. **R.M.S. power** is the usual way of describing the output power of any system; it is the product of r.m.s. output voltage and r.m.s. output current to produce output power wattage. (Remember that the r.m.s. — or root mean square — value is 0.707 of the peak value of a sinewave, the peak value being half of the peak-to-peak value as observed on an oscilloscope screen.) The **peak power** is *twice* the r.m.s. value and the **music power** is 1.5 times the r.m.s. value. For example, a 20 W amplifier can be quoted as 20 W r.m.s., or 40 W peak power or 30 W music power. One further complication arises when **available power** is quoted — this is the power delivered by the amplifier, to the speaker system but not necessarily from the speaker output, owing to inevitable losses in the leads and speaker(s).

A loudspeaker with no cabinet produces very small output since the sounds emitted from the front and the rear of the cone cancel out, the phases being in opposition. Most **baffle boards** or speaker cabinets suppress the sound from the rear of the cone by using various techniques — most try to create an **infinite baffle** system which is equivalent to mounting the speaker on an infinitely large baffle board. If the speaker is housed in a stout wooden box filled with absorbent material, these rear sounds will be absorbed. Some cabinets try to route the rear sounds, via **reflex** boards in the cabinet, outwards with the front sounds. These cabinets unfortunately have resonant points at low frequencies and the modern air-tight high compliance units are preferred; high compliance speakers have very flexible cone mountings to allow the cone to move great distances and so produce high bass outputs. My advice is to buy ready built units for any amplifier system, choosing those with the *most pleasing sound*. Testing speakers presents a problem; the best solution is to try each one in your hi-fi room — some suppliers will allow you to do this. Remember that small bookshelf speakers often need a much greater drive power than larger units to produce the same output volume.

Microphones and pick-ups do not have the problems of the loudspeakers, their mechanical details are smaller and simpler, they handle much less power, and so the frequency responses are more acceptable. Most good microphones and pick-ups have defined frequency responses which can be matched easily to a preamplifier circuit. The impedances of these devices do vary, however, and the circuits of chapter 3 should allow a choice to be made for most

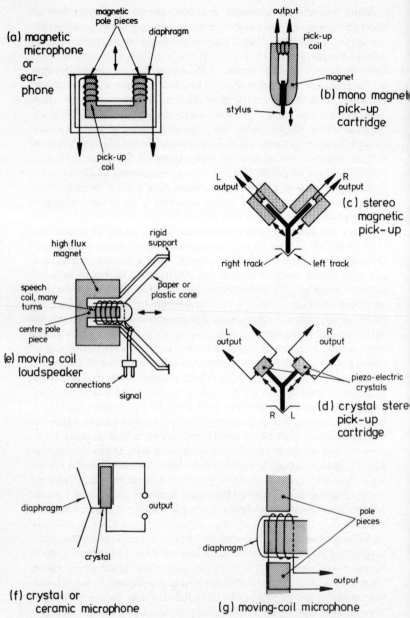

Figure 1.4   Common microphones, pick-ups and speakers

inputs. Impedance values are not too critical — a microphone of 300 Ω impedance can be connected to an amplifier of input impedance of anything between 400 and 200 Ω without the listener detecting this difference.

The devices shown in figure 1.4 can be briefly described as follows.

Magnetic microphone (a) — an electro-magnetic device similar to the loudspeaker where the **diaphragm** moves with sound vibrations to produce an alternating current in the fixed pick-up coil. A strong permanent magnet supplies the magnetic field. These microphones have *low* output impedance and a good frequency response; they can also be used for sound output as miniature loudspeakers, for example, in headphone sets. When used as headphones, watch the amplifier output power — these pick-up coils can only handle small currents, but the insertion of a series resistor or 100 Ω or so will safely limit the current.

Mono magnetic pick-up cartridge (b). The **stylus** replaces the diaphragm of the magnetic microphone and, as it moves along the record groove, the vibrations are converted into output current variations with similar properties to the magnetic microphone.

Stereo magnetic pick-up (c). *Two* such pick-up coils are carefully positioned at 45° to the stereo stylus so that the vibrations on the left and right grooves are mechanically transmitted to the appropriate pick-up coil. Careful design ensures that the cross-talk distortion between left and right signals is minimal. The electrical properties are similar to the magnetic microphone. These pick-ups are heavier than crystal or ceramic types because of the internal magnet; weight compensation must therefore be included in the pick-up arm to give only the required few grams' weight of the stylus in the groove.

Crystal stereo pick-up (d). If a piece of **quartz** crystal (a **piezo-electric** material) is subjected to mechanical stress (given a good thump), a voltage appears across the ends of the crystal. The stylus of this pick-up is positioned so that the vibrations in the left and right sides of the groove are transmitted at 45° to the appropriate quartz crystal, as shown. The cross-talk distortion is again minimised. The output voltage of this pick-up is up to 1 V, which avoids the need for a high gain preamplifier. The frequency response, however, is worse than the magnetic pick-up, with less bass and more treble response. The output impedance is *very high*, which means that the output leads pick up a lot of hum interference, which is not a problem with low impedance pick-ups and microphones. Screened cable should be used for connections. **Ceramic** pick-ups operate in a similar way to crystal but their output frequency response is slightly better.

Moving-coil loudspeaker (e). This type of speaker is used in most audio systems, the rest are electrostatic or horn types. Electro-static speakers deliver excellent sound quality and volume but they require a high voltage drive and very careful positioning in the room. Horn-speakers, using the horn as an impedance-matching device, provide a very large audio output. All types use the basic (electro-mechanical) electrical-to-mechanical conversion described earlier, although the diaphragm or cone varies in construction. Some modern 'flat' speakers use corrugated plastics sheets as the cones to reduce the over-all depth. The moving-coil speaker can also be used as a microphone for, say, an intercom system (chapter 4) although the speech coil should have higher impedance, 35 or 70 Ω, for this pur-pose. Headphones normally use miniature loudspeaker units in preference to the magnetic microphone because of their better frequency response and output.

Crystal or ceramic microphone (f). The diaphragm is connected directly to one end of the piezo-electric crystal, as shown, with the large output being picked up as high impedance across the crystal. The properties are very similar to the stereo magnetic pick-up. These microphones are low-priced and require little preamplification.

Moving-coil microphone (g). A microphone or pick-up can also be constructed, as shown, where the entire coil moves rather than just the diaphragm. The principle is the reverse of the loudspeaker — these microphones or pick-ups are more compact than magnetic ones, with excellent frequency response at low impedance.

There are very many more types of microphone, such as the **carbon** microphone found in telephone handsets (see later) and the **electret** microphone used in cassette tape recorders. The electret is a form of capacitor microphone requiring (like the electrostatic loud-speaker) a polarising voltage, which can be a little inconvenient to produce. They do, however, produce very good quality sound, as do the **ribbon** microphones which use a thin aluminium ribbon as the diaphragm in a moving-coil microphone. The types shown in figure 1.4 are the most common and they are well suited to the circuits of this book.

1.3 General Amplifier Requirements

This chapter has outlined the requirements for a good quality audio amplifier to

(1) **match** the **input device characteristics** — input level, input impedance and frequency response

(2) **match** the **output device characteristics**, usually a loud-speaker with its output power rating and impedance

(3) **maintain** an **audio frequency response** from 30 Hz to 20 kHz or beyond.

Additional requirements vary according to the application but normally include the following:

(4) **Tone controls** for bass, middle and treble adjustments to suit the loudspeaker characteristics and surroundings or merely for

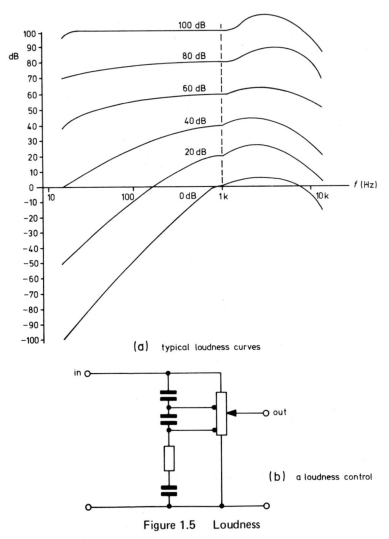

(a) typical loudness curves

(b) a loudness control

Figure 1.5   Loudness

personal choice. Filters are often included for such distortion as tape hiss, record scratches, mains hum, the variations of the ear's response with volume (loudness control), and so on. Every listener has preferences for the types of sound that are most pleasing; tone control circuits should satisfy most different tastes.

(5) A **loudness control**, referred to above, which corrects for the ear response (see figure 1.5). The ear hears all audio frequencies with equal volume *only* when the sound is very loud. If the volume is reduced by 40 dB, 60 dB, and so on, the intensity at high and low frequencies falls until, at very low volume, the bass is almost inaudible. Try this on your audio system. Many amplifiers use a loudness correction circuit as shown or a loudness switch or they centre-tap the volume control via a capacitor to chassis to boost bass and treble at low volume. The simple method merely involves the manual adjustment of bass and treble to suit the listener, but this will change with volume settings. Hi-fi perfectionists often assume that, because they set all tone controls to produce a **flat** frequency response, they are hearing true hi-fi; they do not realise that their two ears are distorting the over-all response of the system.

(6) **Scratch, rumble and tape hiss filters** to eliminate scratch noise on records, rumble noise due to motor vibrations on record player and tape recorder decks and the tape hiss of cassette players. Electronic noise suppression is often used in cassette players, this will be referred to in chapter 2.

(7) **Stereo adjustments** such as balance and left/right tone correction to balance the two channels perfectly.

(8) Other optional refinements, often unnecessary, such as: speaker switches for left, right or left/right through both speakers; power VU meters; quadra switches for pseudo-quadra (see chapter 4); click stops on the rotating controls; individual filters for selected frequencies, usually via a maze of slide controls; monitor output volume; peak overload detector (see chapter 5), and so on.

Chapter 2 applies these properties to a typical audio system.

2
Audio Amplifiers

The circuits of chapters 3 and 4 form the basis of an audio amplifier system as outlined in figure 2.1. The choice of circuit depends on the application — a simple intercom, baby alarm or for filling a large concert hall, for amplifying microphone signals or synthesiser sounds (chapter 5), or merely for the enjoyment of constructing the circuits and investigating their properties. This chapter uses the data collected from chapter 1 and applies them to the design aspects of the amplifiers to be found in the following chapters.

2.1 Types of Audio Amplifier

The block diagram of figure 2.1 identifies a large number of amplifier circuits for a typical audio system, the function of each block being as follows.

Equalisation networks match the impedance and amplitude characteristics of the input device, usually with a passive circuit of resistors and capacitors. These circuits are usually switched via a front panel selector along with the frequency correction (equalisation) circuits (see below).

Input preamplifier. A degree of high gain amplification is necessary in the early stages of amplification to compensate for the losses

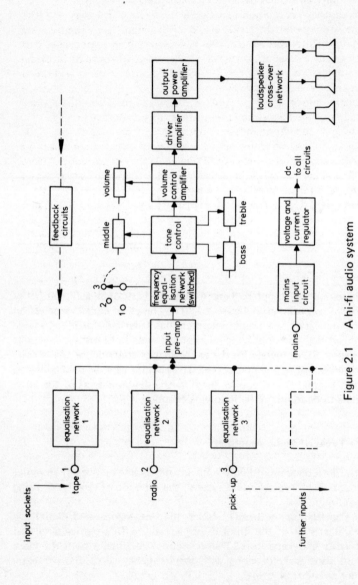

Figure 2.1   A hi-fi audio system

introduced in the various filter and equalisation networks. A low noise high gain stage is used with a flat frequency response.

Frequency equalisation network (switched) corrects for the frequency response differences from various inputs via an active filter circuit which boosts or cuts the bass or treble as appropriate. It is usual to use a single transistor feedback circuit with switched correction components as shown. Discs and cassettes require additional frequency correction (see section 2.4).

Tone controls — bass, middle and treble — form additional filter circuits to cut or boost these frequencies to suit the listener.

Volume control amplifier is positioned at the end of this input chain so that noise introduced by the input stages is cut **down** by the volume control along with the signal. If the volume control were at the input, the noise introduced by the following stages would reach the output amplifier at full amplitude and reduce the signal-to-noise ratio. This stage usually incorporates a further high gain amplifier whose gain is controlled either by remote control (see chapter 3) or via a control through which the audio signal travels, the latter being the normal method before the introduction of the electronic attenuator.

Driver amplifier. The output transistor(s) require considerable current drive and so this stage converts the audio input signal of about 1 V into a current signal of several 100 mA. At the same time it sets the dc levels of the output transistor(s), which are very critical indeed (see chapter 4). A medium power transistor is used.

Output power amplifier. This is a current amplifier which drives the loudspeaker with several watts of power. The design of this stage is complex since frequency response, distortion, gain stabilisation, temperature stability, protection of the output under fault conditions, high efficiency and output loading are all considered in the design. Several amperes of audio signal may feed the loudspeaker and this creates problems of heat dissipation and circuit protection.

Loudspeaker cross-over network. Chapter 1 mentioned that the bass speakers cannot handle treble frequencies; similarly treble speakers cannot handle bass frequencies. Cross-over networks are placed between the amplifier and the speaker to route the appropriate section of the frequency response to either a bass, middle or treble speaker, thereby avoiding the cone of a tweeter being propelled across the living room floor when a giant pipe organ begins to play. The frequencies can be split into two or three with the cross-over frequencies being adjusted accordingly in circuits of chapter 4.

Mains input circuit. A very simple power supply circuit is used with transformer, rectifier diodes and smoothing capacitor. The current capacity of these components is important, however, to avoid overheating by the excessive currents, sometimes up to 6 or 10 A. Safety is of utmost importance in this circuit, this being the only place, except in disco circuits, where 240 V mains are present. Fusing and correct switching and earthing are essential to avoid nasty surprises.

Voltage and current regulator. The final circuit in the system is not always required in power systems but is often used in medium and low powered audio circuits to ensure that the output voltage and/or current are stabilised at the nominal value. High gain circuits are very prone to gain fluctuation and instability when the supply rail rises or falls in voltage and so supply stabilisation is preferred. Output power amplifiers are not so prone to variations, they are more concerned with adequate current input from the mains input. This circuit often includes short-circuit protection, and limits hum to the amplifier via the supply rail.

2.2 Amplifier Frequency Responses

Chapter 1 outlined the response required of the audio system and this section describes two more aspects of amplifier response associated with complex sounds. Musical instruments and virtually any sound, such as those shown in figure 2.2, produce very *complex* waveforms. **Tuning forks** are one of the few sources of pure sinewaves, other sounds involve the basic sinewave (the fundamental) but add an infinite number of **harmonics** in different proportions to create the complex waveshapes. Reference is made in chapter 4 to a squarewave, which contains the fundamental and proportions of all the odd harmonics; this serves as a useful test signal. It is the harmonics which give the sound its characteristic quality and which must all be amplified if true hi-fi is heard. Unfortunately no audio system can amplify frequencies up to infinity and a compromise is reached with amplifiers reaching 20, 50 or 100 kHz.

Despite these limitations the ear can perceive higher harmonics by virtue of the **mixing** effect of lower harmonics (see figure 2.2). If two tuning forks are sounded together at frequencies of f_1 and f_2, then *four* resultant frequencies will be heard, namely $f_1, f_2, f_2 - f_1$, $f_2 + f_1$. If we assume that the amplifier cannot amplify $f_2 + f_1$ but it can amplify f_1 and f_2 individually, then this same mixing will also take place in the ear after the amplifier has done its work. The hi-fi property of the sound is partly replaced, therefore, and frequencies beyond 20 kHz are heard. Unfortunately, these same $f_1 + f_2$ frequencies themselves mix to form even more complex harmonics

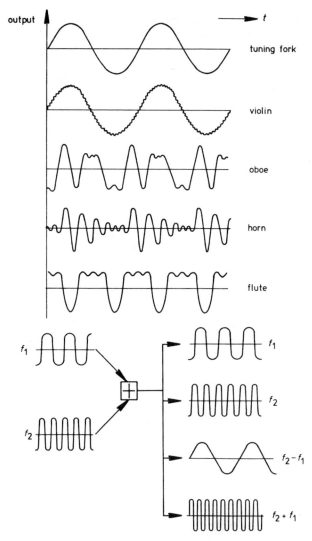

Figure 2.2   Complex sounds

which will not be amplified and so an amplifier with very high band-width is preferred.

A similar process occurs with the lower frequencies, the **difference** frequency being heard as a difference harmonic $f_2 - f_1$. This can be tested on a cheap transistor radio whose loudspeaker, because of its design, cannot possibly produce bass frequencies. Higher harmonics can, however, be amplified and this same mixing is carried out by the ear which mixes them in the same way to produce bass notes. The bass is not as loud as it should be but is there all the same.

The second consideration is the **RIAA recording response** (Record Industry Association of America) shown in figure 2.3a. This is flat for several periods but rises between 100 Hz and 500 Hz and between

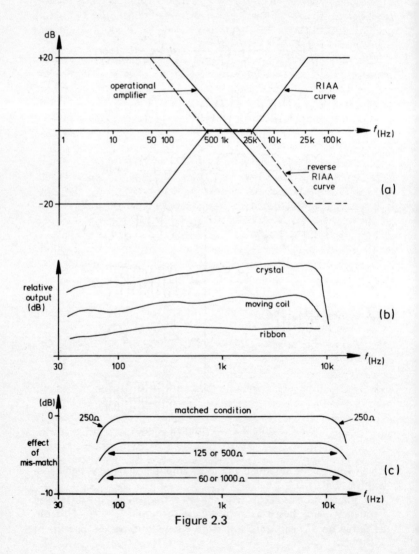

Figure 2.3

2.5 kHz and 25 kHz. The reason for this increased treble response involves the signal-to-noise ratio of the system. Most noise occurs above 2.5 kHz and so if this is boosted on the record along with the signal, when the amplifier cuts the gain with a reverse RIAA response as shown, the noise is considerably reduced. The over-all effect on the signal frequencies is a perfectly flat response. It is a simple matter to produce an amplifier with this reverse RIAA response (see chapter 3) and one amplifier with a very near response is the **741 operational amplifier** which is often used as an audio preamplifier. The 741 has a gain of 100 dB with very high input impedance and low output impedance but costs just a few pence.

One final point to make is that any electro-magnetic device produces an output which varies (a) in signal level with rise in frequency and (b) in proportion to the playing speed of the record or cassette.

A simple mathematical formula $E = -L \ di/dt$ shows this effect, where E is the induced voltage, L the inductance of the pick-up coil and di/dt the rate of change of current.

This too produces a rising treble response which must be corrected in the amplifier. Readers may be aware of the fact that tapes played at 15 in./s sound better than those played at lower speeds. Cassette decks overcome this problem by reducing the head gap width — but all this is leaving the world of electronic circuits behind. The moving-coil pick-up response of figure 2.3b shows this slight rise; the mechanical construction limits the high end of the response. Ribbon microphones are not used as pick-ups but their response can be seen to be very good.

2.3 Amplifier Output Power

Most hi-fi owners have amplifier systems whose output power is *far greater* than necessary. Hi-fi salesmen pride themselves in selling high power amplifiers at low cost but they do not point out the problems that arise with high power amplification. These include increased heat dissipation, higher distortion, higher noise, more hum, more expensive and larger loudspeakers, larger power supplies (more costly) and, finally, more annoyance to the neighbours. A normal living room is adequately served by a moderate 10 + 10 W system; a small hall by a 20 + 20 W system and a large concert hall by a 50 + 50 W system. There is no need at all to install 50 W amplifiers in a living room because only 3 W are necessary for normal listening, with provision for 5 or 6 W for loud passages — remember the possible damage to your ears!

2.4 Filter Applications and Equalisation

Equalisation has already been mentioned, but it is interesting to note the likely attenuation when a bad mismatch occurs — see figure 2.3c. The frequency response can be seen to deteriorate as the mismatch gets worse, with the gain naturally decreasing as the impedance rises or falls from 250 Ω. Connecting the wrong pick-up to an amplifier or connecting the wrong loudspeaker produces this effect. Input circuits are, however, corrected by the equalisation circuits found in chapter 3.

Filter circuits can take two forms, **acceptor** filters to boost the output at predetermined frequencies or **rejector** filters to reduce the output; both are used in audio amplifiers. Rejectors can reduce tape hiss, scratch noise, hum or any unwanted whistles. Acceptors are used in tone control circuits described before, or they can be used in synthesiser circuits to add colour to the generated noises (see chapter 5). The organ circuit of chapter 7 uses filters to produce the characteristic organ sounds from a rough squarewave input, the filtering of the right frequencies being used to shape a squarewave into any wanted sound. Disco circuits are driven from bass, middle and treble acceptor filters to drive the sound-to-light thyristor/triac circuits of chapter 6.

Stereo radio deserves a mention here since every stereo radio transmission, using **multiplex encoding** (beyond the scope of this book unfortunately), adds the stereo signal to the existing mono FM signal, transmitted on the VHF bands. Stereo radio is very susceptible to noise interference at treble frequencies and so a similar boosting at treble frequencies takes place to RIAA correction. It is called **pre-emphasis** which takes place at the transmitter. The receiver has a **de-emphasis** circuit (after the decoder) which reduces the treble output along with the noise; the over-all audio response is very flat (we hope). Cassette recorder systems use either the **Dolby** system, which again uses this same treble boost/cut on recording and playing back, or the **dynamic noise limiter**, which senses quiet passages on playback and filters the high frequencies (and noise) from them. Loud passages are left alone, nothing happens on recording. Low noise cassettes and a combination of these systems and hi-fi electronics has brought the cassette recorder into the hi-fi market along with record players and other equipment.

2.5 Amplifier Construction

The following section must be read before embarking on the construction of a full audio system since hints are given on earthing, power supplies, component layout, heat dissipation and a large number of other important items.

The first point involves hum within the system. This can arrive at the output in many ways as follows.

(1) Through earth currents which travel round the various earth circuits looking for the point of lowest potential. These are minimised by connecting all earths from all boards and components to just *one* chassis point as seen in figure 2.4a. *All* earth currents must now flow only to this point, the same point as mains earth, for safety reasons.

(2) Through voltages induced into input leads from the magnetic field of the mains transformer. These 50 Hz signals create a few microvolts or millivolts of hum in the high gain inputs and so are amplified to produce very large hum outputs. The position of the mains transformer is critical — it must be well away from the input leads, sockets and controls as seen in figure 2.4b. If trouble persists then carefully rotate the transformer until the hum disappears. Keep the mains input lead, switch, fuse and mains indicator away from these same places as well, because they too can cause hum. The ultimate solution is, of course, to use battery supplies but this will demand a regular supply of car batteries or accumulators to deliver the 30 V or so at 2 A or more.

(3) Through insufficient smoothing of the power supply(s) or inadequate regulation. The supplies described should have adequate smoothing via a few thousand μF capacitor, but this can be increased if necessary; alternatively a *CRC* filter can be formed by splitting the capacitor into two and placing a high power low value (few Ω) resistor in series with the dc output, the capacitors being either side of the resistor. The regulator should reduce the hum to a negligible amount.

With regard to the power supply, a few more hints are useful. Switch the mains input via a **double-pole switch** for safety reasons. A single-pole switch may leave the entire circuit live. A **mains indicator** such as a neon is useful, as is a low voltage lamp on the dc output. Ensure that the output supply leads can carry the necessary current without **overheating**. If they are too thin they will heat up and, if the insulation melts, a short to chassis could occur, starting a fire. Each circuit should try to use the same supply voltage(s) so that series dropper resistors are not needed. Most preamplifier circuits will operate over a range of supply voltages, as will most push—pull output amplifiers.

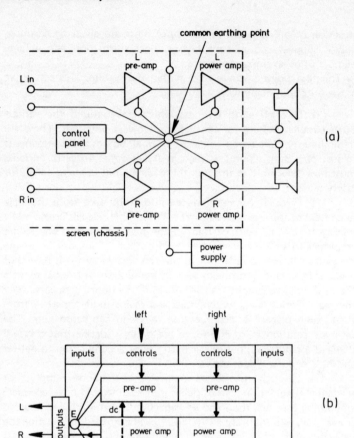

Figure 2.4   Earthing and layout

The construction of the system should start with the power supply, which should first be thoroughly tested. The regulator circuit, if used, should follow and then the output amplifier. These now comprise a fully operational audio amplifier to which all the other preamplifiers and noise makers can be connected. It also helps if each individual circuit is built on to its separate board, each board being installed as in figure 2.4, with colour-coded leads to the rest of the circuit and a neat wiring layout. Do not have leads longer than necessary, particularly power leads and coaxial leads. Identification with self-adhesive labels helps fault tracing, both of leads and inputs and outputs. *Neatness is of the utmost importance* in audio amplifier construction. Coaxial input leads should be earthed at each end to the sockets and the amplifier input (remember the common earthing point as well).

Many circuits have components which heat up and so require heat-sinking. **Heat sinks** can be attached to these components and they can be placed in an airy position in the cabinet for adequate circulation. Alternatively these components can be mounted on the outside metal chassis, which will also serve to screen outside interference. The components should normally be insulated from the chassis using mica washers smeared with silicone grease to give good thermal contact between the component and chassis. It is good practice to check with an ohmmeter to see if any shorts to chassis are present before switching the power on.

When testing audio circuits test each circuit in turn. If everything is connected up and then the mains switched on, every transistor or IC can be damaged in one millisecond by a careless wiring fault — an expensive business. Test the power supply, then the amplifier, then the other circuits, remembering always to have the loudspeakers connected. Sophisticated test gear is not necessary, just a very simple multimeter and an audio source such as a small transistor radio or cassette player. The audio signal can be tapped via a 0.1 μF capacitor from the volume control, remembering to connect the chassis together. Each section can now be tested starting from the output and working back to the input. Don't be too upset if you have trouble — no one is perfect. One fault that is often found is inadequate **decoupling** of the supply rail to each circuit, particularly preamplifiers. The addition of a series few hundred Ω and 25 μF to chassis should cure the trouble.

3
Preamplifiers

The circuits in this chapter will accept a variety of input signals from microphones, pick-ups, radio, and so on, with a wide range of input impedances and levels. To help you make a choice, table 3.1 indexes this chapter.

3.1 Simple Transistor Circuits

These circuits use up to three common transistors and the constructional details are given for several circuits at the end of this chapter, starting at figure 3.17.

3.1.1 Single Transistor Circuits

Four such amplifiers are shown in figures 3.1 and 3.2a, each having distinct properties. The circuit of figure 3.1a comprises a transistor connected in *common base* mode to provide low input impedance and high output impedance for matching low impedance microphones or pick-ups to an output amplifier. This circuit is one of the few to use a germanium *pnp* transistor; its construction is shown in figure 3.17 where it can be seen that the over-all size is very small, allowing the circuit and battery to be inserted into the casing of a microphone

Table 3.1 Amplifier index

Figure	Input	Gain	Frequency Response	Trans- istors	ICs	Output
3.1a	low Z*	1	flat	1	—	high Z
3.1b	medium	20	treble boost	1	—	medium
3.1c	carbon microphone	high	poor	1	—	4–15 Ω
3.2a	1.5 kΩ	46 dB	27 Hz–120 kHz	1	—	5.6 kΩ
3.2b	330 Ω	66 dB	20 Hz–32 kHz	2	—	820 Ω
3.2c	3.9 kΩ	76 dB	35 Hz–35 kHz	2	—	4.7 kΩ
3.2d	3.3 MΩ	very high	flat	2	—	1 kΩ
3.2e	200 to 600 Ω	46 dB	50 Hz–100 kHz	2	—	100 Ω
3.2f	100 kΩ	20 dB	flat (1.5 V)	2	—	medium
3.3a	100 kΩ, vol. control	high	flat	2	—	medium
3.3b	15 kΩ	agc	flat	3	—	medium
3.4	switched (3)	switched	switched	3	—	low
3.5	low Z, transformer	high	flat	3	—	low
3.6	various (5)	very high	flat	—	1	500 mV
3.7	magnetic pick-up	high	RIAA correction	—	1	low
3.8a	low Z microphone	100	741 response	—	1	low
3.8b	ceramic pick-up	1	741 response	—	1	low
3.8c	10 kΩ	10	tone control	—	1	low
3.8d	crystal pick-up	9	flat	—	1	low
3.8e	medium, 10 kΩ	5 dB	bass boost	1	1	low
3.8f	10 kΩ	1	tunable filter	—	2	low
3.8g	500 kΩ	1000	fuzz	—	1	low
3.9	mixer inputs	1	flat	—	1	low
3.10	mixer inputs	2	flat	—	1	low
3.11	3.9 kΩ	1	scratch/rumble	—	1	low
3.12	330 kΩ	2	tone control	—	2	low
3.14	medium	10 dB	tone control	2	—	low
3.15	17 kΩ	12 dB	flat	—	1	260 Ω
3.16	17 kΩ(3)	12 dB	tone control	—	3	260 Ω(3)

* Z equals 'impedance'

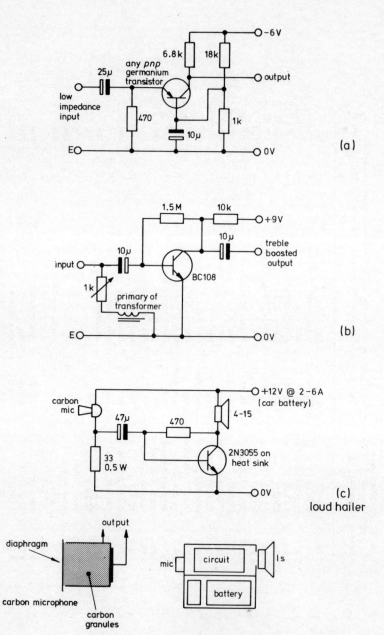

Figure 3.1   Single transistor amplifiers

or pick-up — this prevents the leads being too long and susceptible to noise and hum pick-up.

The second circuit (figure 3.1b) provides **treble boost** and is built around a **common emitter** BC108 amplifier. The primary of *any* transformer will suit this circuit — trial and error will give the required boost. Don't throw away a damaged transformer — the undamaged winding can be used for this circuit. This circuit is intended for systems where treble response is poor, for example, speaker systems without a tweeter, poor quality pick-ups or public-address units which boost the treble rather than bass since high frequency speech is easier to understand than boomy bass speech. Portable public-address systems such as a hand-held **loud hailer** can use just one power transistor to deliver several watts into a loudspeaker such as that in figure 3.1c. Nickel—cadmium batteries can be used to supply the several amperes for this circuit (over short periods), which uses the ever-powerful 2N3055 transistor. A **carbon microphone** supplies the audio signal since this type of microphone produces a very large output. Carbon microphones are used in telephone handsets and consist of compressed carbon granules in a metal case. As the sound waves hit the diaphragm, the density, and therefore the resistance, of the granules changes, and, with a series battery supply provided via the 33 Ω resistor, a large output current can be fed to the 2N3055 for amplification. This transistor will require a heat sink — careful design will result in a very compact unit as shown, with the outer metal case acting as the heat sink. The microphone should be sound-insulated from the speaker by pointing one to the front and the other to the back.

The final circuit in this section is a general-purpose high gain low noise preamplifier with a relatively flat response (see figure 3.2a). Input and output impedance are medium, so ceramic or crystal microphones or pick-ups can use this circuit, provided a series resistor of 100 kΩ is placed at the input.

3.1.2 Further Transistor Preamplifiers
The remaining amplifiers in figures 3.2 to 3.5 provide greater amplification for a wide selection of inputs — this is necessary to compensate for the losses in equalisation networks and tone controls. The circuits use **dc coupling** throughout which is to be preferred since there are no series capacitors or transformers to limit the frequency response.

Series capacitors change their reactance according to the formula $X_C = 1/(2\pi f C)\,\Omega$, transformers change their reactance according to $X_L = 2\pi f L\ \Omega$, where X represents the reactance, f the frequency and

C and *L* the capacitance (farads) and inductance (henrys) respectively.

The only places where series capacitors or transformers are used are at the input and output where they are inserted for **dc isolation** between different circuits. The power amplifiers of chapter 4 sometimes use coupling capacitors to the loudspeaker.

The circuits in figure 3.2 provide various input and output

(a) 46 dB,
27 Hz – 120 kHz

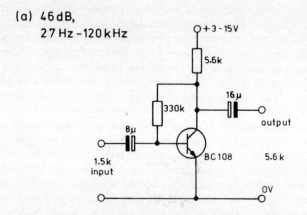

(b) 66 dB,
20 Hz – 32 kHz

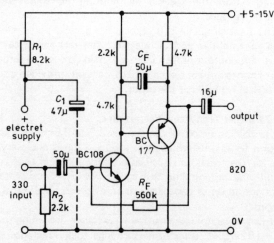

Figure 3.2   Preamplifier circuits

(c) 76dB,
   35Hz –35kHz

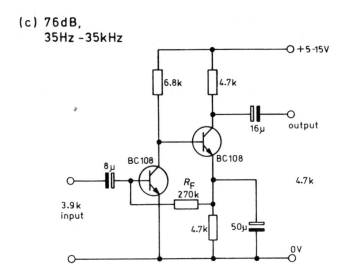

(d) bootstrap,
   gain = $R \times h_{fe1} \times h_{fe2}$

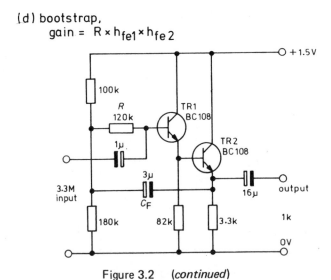

Figure 3.2   (*continued*)

(e) 46 dB, 50Hz–100kHz low noise.

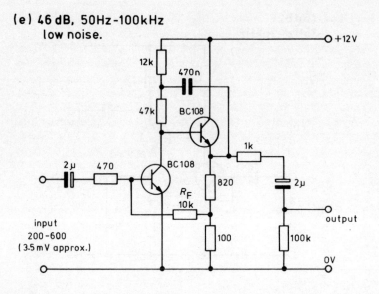

(f) 20 dB, 1.5V supply

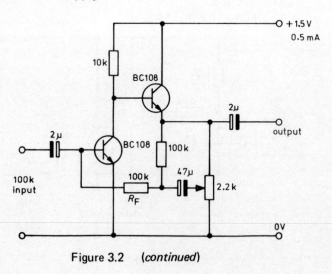

Figure 3.2 (*continued*)

impedances for low input/low output (figure 3.2b); low input/high output (figure 3.2e); medium input/medium output (figure 3.2c); high input/low output (figure 3.2d); medium input/low output (figure 3.2f). Feedback components are included in all circuits to provide **negative feedback** and so flatten the frequency responses. The **open-loop** gain, with no feedback, is very high indeed (several thousand) and this is sacrificed to flatten the response and stabilise gain, as well as greatly reducing the over-all noise and distortion. The feedback components are shown as R_F and/or C_F in each circuit, the remaining components serving for biasing or emitter stabilisation use.

A few comments follow on the design aspects of these circuits. Circuit 3.2b has an optional **electret** supply formed from R_1 and C_1. The electret microphone normally has an internal FET amplifier which transforms the high capacitor impedance down to a low impedance of a few hundred Ω. R_2 acts as the load for this FET amplifier, with R_1, C_1 and R_2 being omitted for normal magnetic inputs. A suggested layout is shown in figure 3.17.

The **bootstrap** circuit 3.2d is a standard design for providing *very high* input impedance in any amplifier. The feedback capacitor deceives the input into thinking that the input impedance is much higher than it is; it works very well. Circuit 3.2e has a very low noise figure because of the large amount of feedback used. This can be made even lower if BC549 and BC547 transistors are used for the first and second stages respectively, along with metal film resistors. An input of 4 mV will produce an output of 820 mV; 50 mV will produce 10 V.

Circuit 3.2f will run from a small 1.5 V dry cell which makes it perfect for inclusion in the case of a microphone or distant source. The 2.2 kΩ preset will control the gain to suit the microphone and the circuit also runs from two dry cells in series, thereby giving very long life with only 0.5 mA supply; below 1 V the circuit gives up altogether.

A general-purpose preamplifier with good audio response and gain of around 60 dB is shown in figure 3.3a; construction details are given in figure 3.18. Two feedback loops are incorporated, one in each stage, via the 220 kΩ and 15 kΩ resistors to flatten the response. Small 100 pF and 18 pF capacitors are placed across the transistors, as in many stages such as this, to cancel the internal transistor capacitance which would limit the high frequency response. The circuit in figure 3.3b behaves like a single transistor preamplifier around TR2 with about 25 dB gain. The gain is automatically controlled by an agc circuit (**automatic gain control**) which

(a)

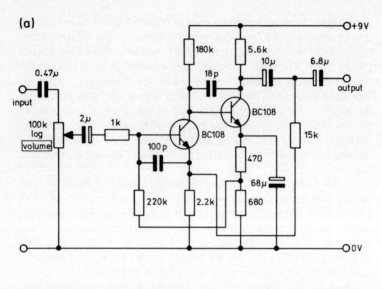

(b)

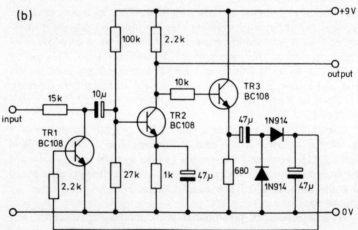

Figure 3.3   General-purpose preamplifiers

keeps the output level constant for a wide range of input signal levels. TR3 amplifies the output signal which is rectified and smoothed to be fed as a dc bias to TR1 which acts as a variable resistor across the input signal to TR2. An increase in input level generates more dc bias to TR1 base to reduce TR1 collector—emitter resistance and hence reduce the input accordingly. This circuit is suitable for input signals up to 1 V and, with a low input impedance of a few hundred Ω, is suitable for intercom use. Alternatively this circuit doubles as a **sound compressor** which always gives a constant output level. Sound compressors are used in recording studios to ensure that sound levels on records and cassettes are always constant, in both quiet and loud passages. More circuits are given in chapter 5.

A common circuit design for a multi-input equalisation preamplifier is given in figure 3.4 (layout in figure 3.18). The three-position switch is ganged, section (a) matching the input device and section (b) adjusting the frequency response. **Frequency selective** negative feedback is used, the amplifier having sufficient gain to compensate for losses in the filter. One feature of this circuit, which is common to all preamplifier circuits, is the **decoupling** of the supply to the high gain input stage using the 47 kΩ/100 kΩ divider and 6.8 μF capacitor. This filters out any hum or interference on the supply rail and so isolates the input stage from the rest.

The final circuit in this section is designed for special microphones with a **balanced** output. Many low impedance microphones, whose leads are susceptible to hum pick-up, use a **twin balanced output** of two leads plus an earthed screen. Any hum introduced into these leads is cancelled out in the transformer primary, the hum being in antiphase in each half. The transformer is also used to match the amplifier high impedance input as shown in figure 3.5. Here a FET has its resistance adjusted with resistor R to suit a variety of input levels. The signal passes to a conventional dc coupled preamplifier with gain 46 dB, the gain being adjusted with a 5 kΩ preset. The Zener diode ensures that the bias conditions are stable for the preamplifier transistors, the circuit being similar in design to that of figure 3.2e.

3.1.3 Fault-finding in Transistor Amplifiers

Very little need be said about the testing of these circuits since a little knowledge of transistor operation is all that is necessary to establish the approximate voltage levels to be expected. The base of an *npn* transistor should be at a dc level of 0.6 V above its emitter, a *pnp* transistor has its base 0.6 V below the emitter. Under fault conditions this will not be the case; the normal procedure is to test the *output* transistors and, if correct, proceed back along the chain checking each transistor in turn. Complex dc coupled circuits such as those in chapter 4, present problems since every dc level is interlinked. Remember that dc levels cannot pass through capacitors and that stages can be isolated by disconnecting these capacitors (where they

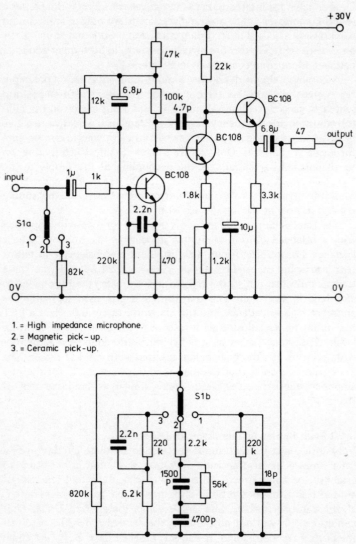

1. = High impedance microphone.
2. = Magnetic pick-up.
3. = Ceramic pick-up.

Figure 3.4   Switched preamplifier

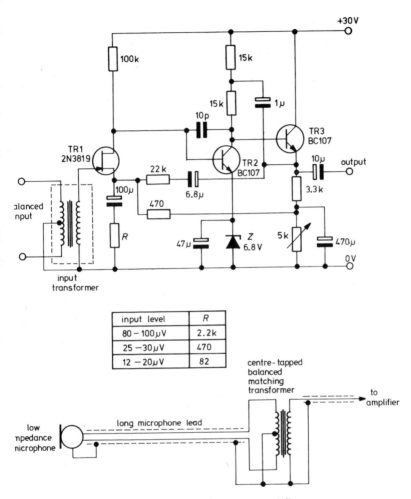

input level	R
80 – 100 μV	2.2k
25 – 30 μV	470
12 – 20 μV	82

Figure 3.5   Microphone preamplifier

appear). In a dc coupled circuit, the shorting of an input base to chassis will turn this transistor off, its collector voltage should rise, its emitter voltage should fall and every other transistor will turn on or off according to the method of connection. The ac signal can be shorted to chassis at any point with a small capacitor. In a circuit such as figure 3.5 the shorting of TR2 base to chassis will turn TR2 off, raising TR3 base voltage which will drive TR3 on hard. The output emitter voltage should now rise and this will upset TR1 voltages accordingly.

It is normal for dc coupled amplifiers to *either work well or not at all*. A common fault is an inoperative transistor; this does not preclude the faults created by a careless constructor, faulty wiring, incorrect connections, poor soldering, wrong board layout, shorting of component leads, wrongly connected inputs or outputs, or lack of a supply voltage. Boards can be checked visually before connection of the supply with a few ohmmeter checks to protect the power supply.

3.2 IC Preamplifier Circuits

Integrated circuit manufacturers often supply suggested circuits for custom-made audio amplifiers; some are described in this section. Other circuits use the common 741 operational amplifier with its 1001 uses, including audio amplification.

The circuit of figure 3.6 should strictly speaking come in section 3.1½ since it is a **hybrid** encapsulated preamplifier circuit, the HY5, using internal transistors and integrated circuits to perform high gain amplification with all the necessary equalisation circuitry and frequency correction. The input equalisation is adjusted by connecting input pin 4 to the appropriate input device via S1a and pin 3 to pin 5, 6, 9 or 10. The HY5 has two amplifier stages, interconnected via the volume control; the second stage comprises a tone control circuit with ±12 dB adjustment at 100 Hz for bass and 10 kHz for treble. The input impedance is nominally 47 kΩ on all inputs except ceramic, although any input works well, at the expense of reduced gain. Distortion is 0.05 per cent at 1 kHz and the signal-to-noise ratio is 68 dB. The supply voltage can be ±16 V to ±50 V at 15 mA with 1 kΩ resistors in series with each lead above 30 V. The magnetic input is RIAA corrected.

This amplifier is *very* reliable and is *highly* recommended for all applications.

A preamplifier which is currently available for RIAA corrected magnetic pick-ups is seen around a LM381 IC in figure 3.7. This is a **stereo preamplifier** with two side-by-side preamplifiers which can be connected in parallel (as shown) or individually. This is an adaptation of an operational amplifier with two inputs, one **inverting** (−) and the other **non-inverting** (+). Two inputs to − and + allow the amplifier to be used as a differential amplifier with uses in synthesiser circuits. The normal connection for audio circuits is to use just one

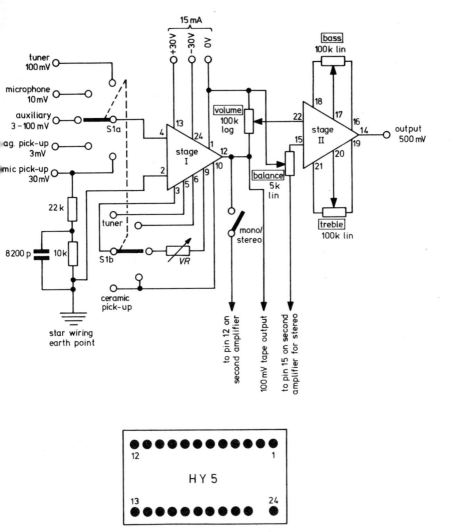

Figure 3.6   Hybrid preamplifier

input, either − or +, with negative feedback applied to the inverting input (shown with the RIAA circuit connected).

The most common operational amplifier is the versatile and cheap 741, shown in figure 3.8. All the circuits up to figure 3.12 use the 741 or any equivalent operational amplifier. Different feedback

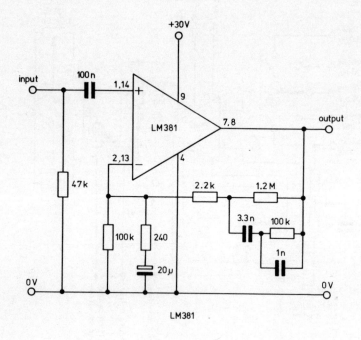

LM381

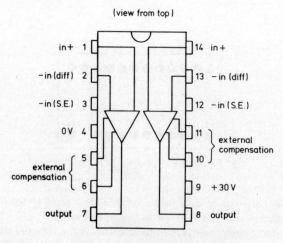

Figure 3.7   RIAA magnetic cartridge amplifier

circuits can be applied to alter the frequency response, the gain or the input and output impedances as follows.

(a) **Microphone amplifier** using an input transformer to match the microphone impedance to the very high 741 input impedance. A balanced input transformer can be used, as in figure 3.5, with a centre-tapped earth. The two resistors provide sufficient feedback for a gain of 100 (40 dB) with relatively low output impedance.

(b) **Ceramic pick-up amplifier** has an input matching circuit with frequency correction, the feedback being 100 per cent and so the gain is unity.

(c) **Tone control amplifier** similar in appearance to that of figure 3.14, where two transistors are substituted for the 741. This method of bass and treble adjustment, called the **Baxandall** circuit and shown in figure 3.13, is very popular; it can be placed anywhere in the series chain of circuits. This circuit introduces considerable loss in gain and should be preceded or followed by a preamplifier. A variation of ±20 dB is possible with each control.

(d) **Crystal pick-up amplifier** with a gain of 9 and necessary frequency compensation.

(e) **Low frequency amplifier** to give bass boost to any circuit. The loss in bass frequencies of many small bookshelf loudspeakers can be corrected by placing this circuit into the appropriate preamplifier; the boost is about 5 dB at 50 Hz, the base bias being formed from the negative supply to the transistor emitter.

(f) **Tunable active filters** can be used to reject any unwanted frequency with great precision. This circuit rejects up to 40 dB at frequencies of 150 Hz to 3 kHz, the filter bandwidth is set by R_2, the frequency by R_1.

(g) **Fuzz boxes** are found in recording studios — they intentionally distort the input signal causing the amplifier to be overdriven and produce second harmonic distortion. Adjustment of the input control sets the gain of the 741, which can have a gain of between 20 and 1000; the optimum setting is found by trial and error. The output components colour the fuzz noise, the output level being set by the volume control shown.

Figure 3.9 shows a typical **mixer circuit** configuration of a 741 or a LM381, point A being called the **summing point** where the input signal currents are added. The input 500 kΩ controls are adjusted by trial and error according to the signal levels and impedances. An alternative 741 circuit is seen in figure 3.10 with a gain of 2 but, unlike the circuit of figure 3.9b, using a *single* supply rail. This method of conversion from dual supply to single supply is common, two 47 kΩ resistors being connected as shown to form a floating

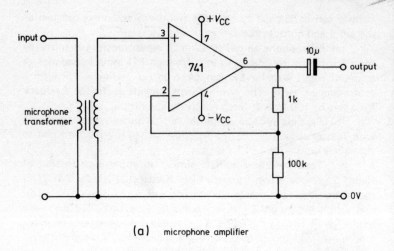

(a)   microphone amplifier

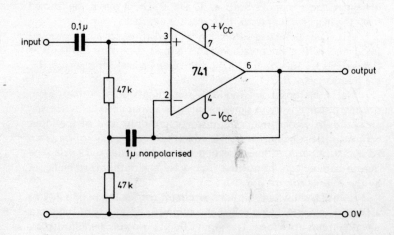

(b)   ceramic pick-up amplifier

Figure 3.8   741 circuits

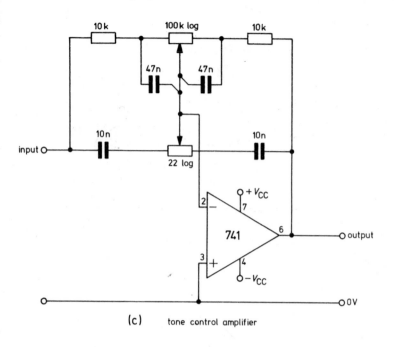

(c)   tone control amplifier

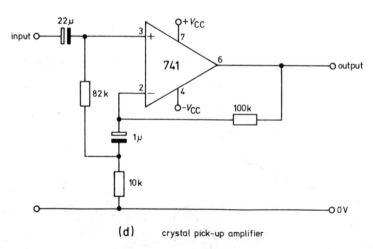

(d)   crystal pick-up amplifier

Figure 3.8   (*continued*)

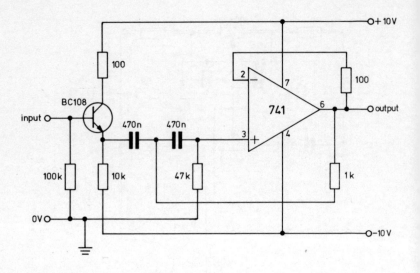

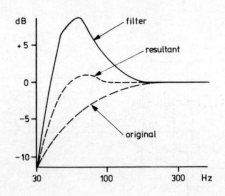

(e) low frequency amplifier

Figure 3.8 (*continued*)

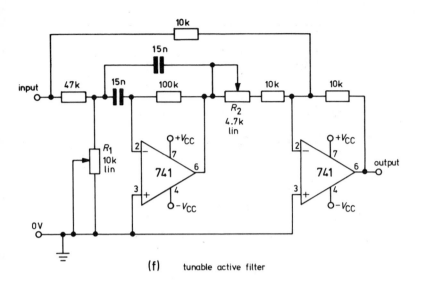

(f)   tunable active filter

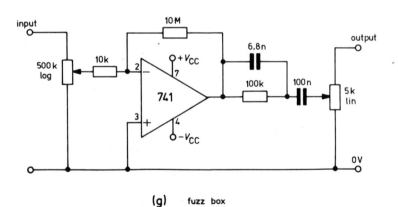

(g)   fuzz box

Figure 3.8   (*continued*)

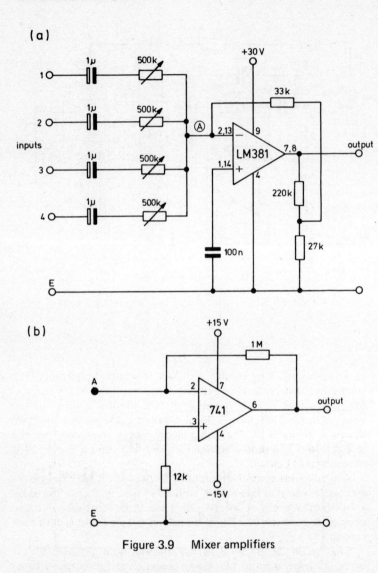

Figure 3.9   Mixer amplifiers

earth for the 741 — this point is decoupled with a capacitor to the new 0 V line. Construction details are shown in figure 3.19, the input capacitors being wired between the sockets and volume controls directly.

Two very common **filter** circuits are shown in figure 3.11, for 3

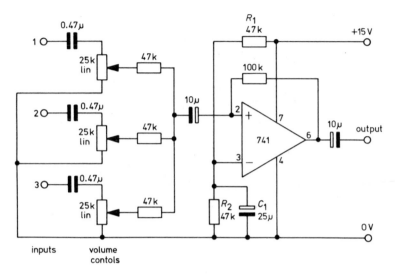

Figure 3.10   Audio mixer using single supply rail

dB rejection at 20 Hz **rumble** and 20 kHz **scratch** frequencies. The circuit uses **Butterworth** low and high pass filters with 18 dB attenuation per octave (complex mathematics is needed to arrive at the values shown). The constructional details for the rumble filter are shown in figure 3.19. The components can be transposed for the scratch filter. The supply voltage can vary between ±3 V and ±18 V as with any 741 circuit.

A simple **tone control** circuit using *three* controls for bass, middle and treble is seen in figure 3.12, with a 741 preamplifier followed by a 741 feedback circuit incorporating the three frequency selective circuits. A variation of ±20 dB boost and cut are possible with each control.

The circuit of figure 3.13 has already been referred to — it includes a **balance** control for stereo operation and an output **volume** control. For stereo operation two such circuits are needed, the bass, treble and volume controls being ganged together for left and right channels.

The circuit of figure 3.14 incorporates necessary amplification as with the earlier 741 circuit to provide ±20 dB of boost and cut; the layout is found on figure 3.20.

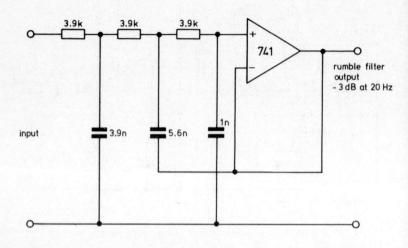

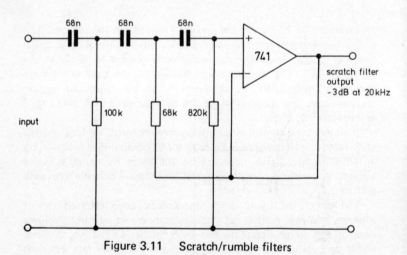

Figure 3.11   Scratch/rumble filters

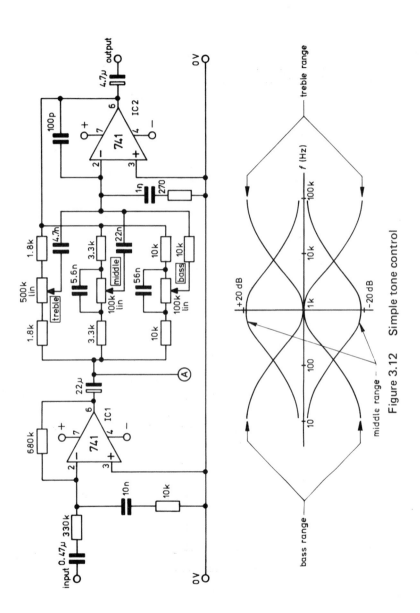

Figure 3.12   Simple tone control

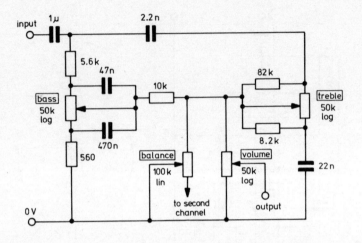

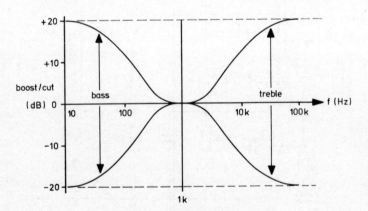

Figure 3.13   Passive tone control

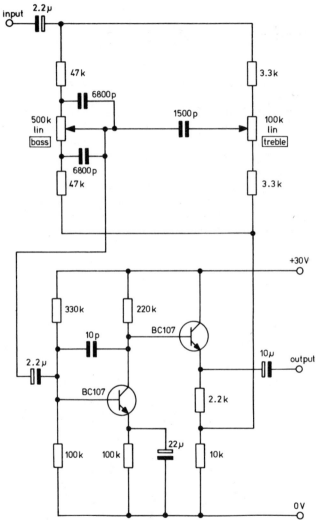

Figure 3.14   Tone control with amplification

One circuit that has revolutionised audio system design is the MC3340P **electronic attenuator** which is a high gain amplifier whose gain is controlled by a **dc bias** rather than the conventional volume control through which the signal normally passes. A dc bias of 3.5 to 6 V is passed to pin 2 or the circuit of figure 3.15 can be connected to give control between −90 dB and +13 dB. The input impedance is 17 kΩ with a maximum input level of 500 mV; the output impedance is 260 Ω.

This circuit can be inserted into any system where volume control (remote if desired) is needed. One such application is illustrated in figure 3.16 where three of these ICs are connected as a **tone control**, one for bass, one for middle and the other for treble. The input capacitors and cut-off capacitors to pin 6 adjust the frequency responses. The construction details are shown in figure 3.21 with three slider controls mounted on the same board as the ICs. An alternative method uses three **remote controlled** potentiometers whose distances from the circuit are unimportant. The big advantage of this circuit is that the control can be isolated from the signal, thereby avoiding noisy controls and long coaxial cables from amplifier to volume control.

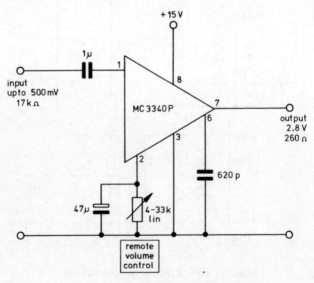

Figure 3.15   Electronic attenuator

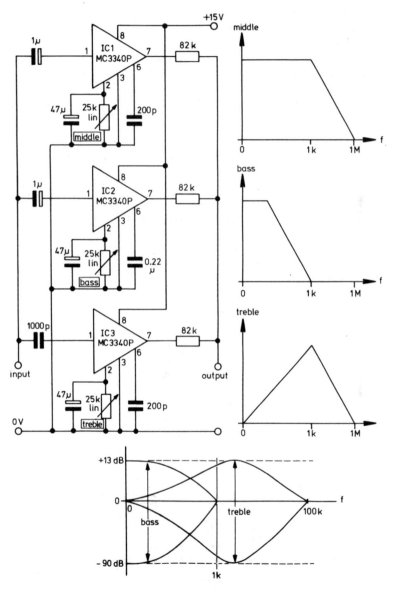

Figure 3.16   Electronic tone control

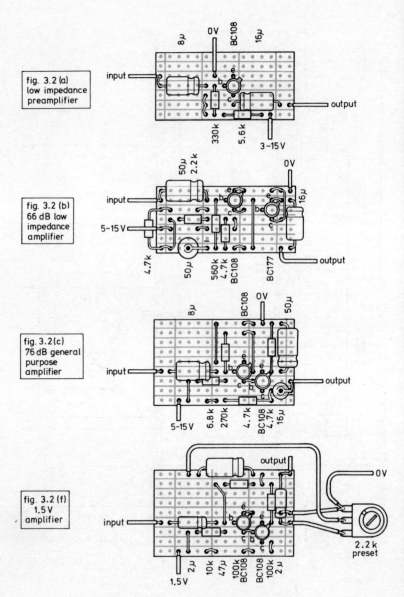

Figure 3.17   Constructional details

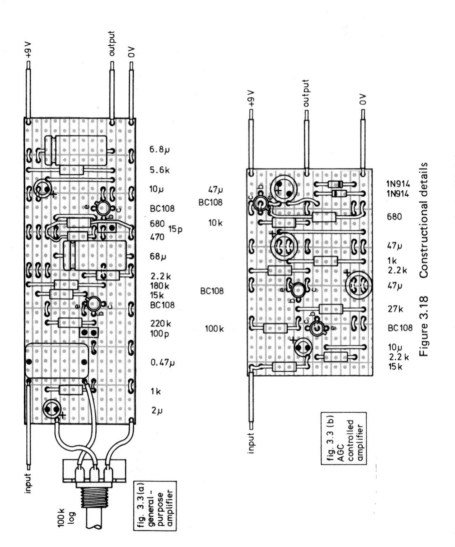

Figure 3.18 Constructional details

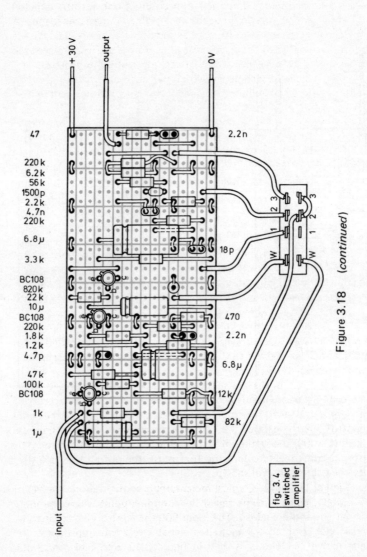

Figure 3.18 (continued)

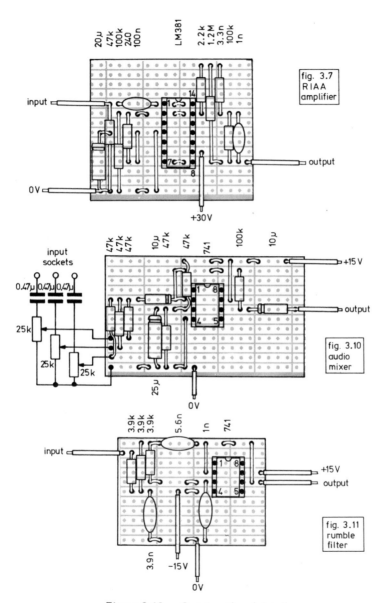

Figure 3.19   Constructional details

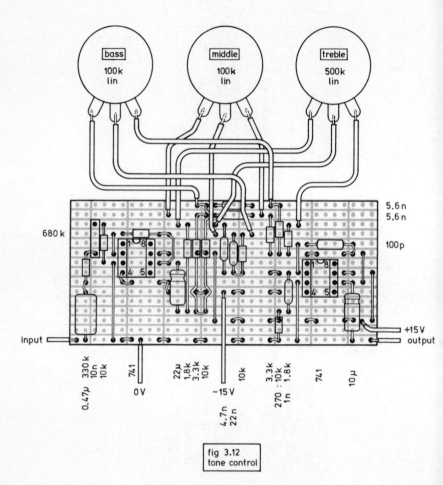

fig 3.12
tone control

Figure 3.20   Constructional details

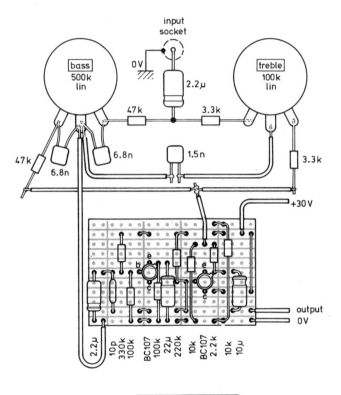

fig. 3.14
tone control amplifier

Figure 3.20   (*continued*)

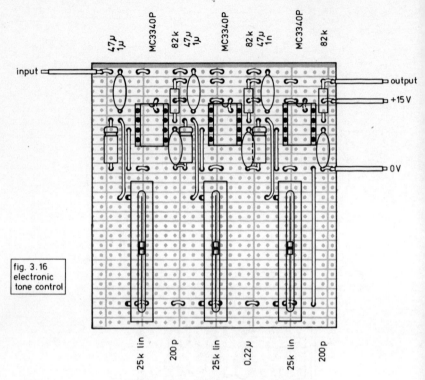

fig. 3.16
electronic
tone control

Figure 3.21   Constructional details

4
Power Amplifiers

The dictionary defines an amplifier as a device which gives greater **loudness**. The circuits in this chapter certainly do this, by accepting the small signals from the preamplifier circuits of chapter 3 of about 500 mV or so, synthesiser or organ circuits from later chapters, or microphone signals direct. The power amplifier supplies sufficient **power** to the loudspeaker to enable the speech coil to move in and out by the required amount.

A **power amplifier** should not be confused with a **voltage** amplifier, which was discussed in chapter 3. Power amplifiers supply currents of up to several amperes and enable the speaker cone to move at frequencies of between 10 Hz and 20 kHz with no distortion or limiting. A speaker cone moves when large currents or a very strong magnetic field, or both, are present, a high voltage being necessary in the amplifier merely to bias the transistors and cause the large currents to be generated.

The amplifier circuit chosen will depend on the **volume** to be filled by the sound, as described in section 2.3. Once an amplifier has been chosen, the output power is fixed and so a loudspeaker with this power rating can be found. To help you make a choice, table 4.1 indexes this chapter.

Table 4.1

Figure	Input	Gain	Transistors	ICs	Output
4.1	high Z	20	2	1	1 W, 15 Ω
4.2	35 Ω	10	2	—	1 W, 35 Ω
4.3	90 kΩ, 400 mV	20	5	—	10 W, 8 Ω
4.4, 4.5	high, crystal	20 dB	—	1	2 W, 8 Ω
4.6	high, L + R	high	—	1	2 + 2 W, 8 + 8 Ω
4.7	high Z	high	—	1	4 W, 2 Ω or 16 W, 16 Ω
4.8	100 kΩ	90 dB	—	1	21 W, 4–8 Ω
4.9	100 kΩ, 500 mV	high	—	1	25 W, 4–16 Ω
4.10	high Z	40 dB	5	1	20 W, 8 Ω
4.11	500 mV	high	7	—	9/20/40/70 W, 8 Ω
4.12, 4.13	1 V	high	4	1	50 or 100 W, 8 Ω

4.1 Simple Transistor Amplifiers up to 10 W

Transistors can be operated in one of several classes, **class A** and **class B** being the usual ones chosen for audio amplifiers. The preamplifier transistors of chapter 3 use class A operation where the input and output waveforms are similar in shape. The fuzz box, on the other hand, distorted the signal and so the amplifier was operated under class AB or B. Class B amplifiers cut the input signal into two so that only *half* the waveshape passes to the output; class AB is somewhere between the two with slight **clipping** of the signal.

The circuits of this chapter use either class A or B, the advantage of class B being the greater utilisation of input power from the power supply and so a greater output is obtained for the same input. The maximum **efficiency** of class A amplifiers is 50 per cent whereas for class B amplifiers it is 78 per cent. This means that class B amplifiers do not waste so much power as class A, dissipating the wasted power in the form of heat. The power supply current is therefore lower also and so the power supply can be physically smaller and cheaper to construct.

An amplifier which is designed to distort the signal may not seem very useful but if two are used in a **push—pull** configuration, one can amplify the top half of the input while the other amplifies the lower half with the two amplified halves being added in the loudspeaker. Figure 4.1 shows a single 1 W push—pull amplifier with all the essential voltage waveforms to illustrate the operation. A 741 acts as input preamplifier to boost the input signal to about 1 V at its output. The gain is calculated from R_F/R_{IN}, as is the case with all operational amplifiers, so the gain of this 741 is 18. The output will have zero dc bias since the 741 runs from a split supply. This signal passes through D1 (which is *forward* biased all the time) and the dc level of the audio signal is raised by 0.6 V since the voltage drop across any silicon diode is 0.6 V. TR1 is biased to *only* amplify signals whose voltage exceeds 0.6 V, whether ac or dc and so only the top half cycle passes to the emitter. Diode D2 does a similar job to the lower half, a *pnp* transistor being biased with −0.6 V to allow negative signals below −0.6 V to be passed to its emitter. Thus it is clear that this output amplifier does *not* voltage amplify, an emitter follower having unity gain or thereabouts. It does, however *current* amplify to drive the loudspeaker speech coil. The two halves of the signal appear at the junction of the two emitter circuits, provided the bias has been set correctly.

Cross-over distortion is often a problem with these circuits, caused by the two halves not meeting exactly. It makes a rasping noise and

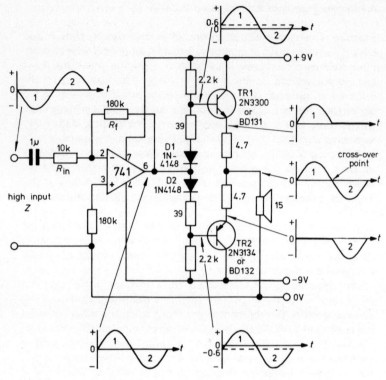

Figure 4.1   Simple 1 W amplifier

later circuits include an adjustment for it. (This form of cross-over distortion must not be confused with the **cross-talk** between left and right channels of a stereo system.) Cross-over distortion can be demonstrated by shorting out D1 or D2, then the sound on the speaker should distort. If distortion is heard anyway, this is due to an unbalance in the push–pull stage, caused by different transistor gains, different diode characteristics or different resistor values.

It will be noticed that the loudspeaker is coupled **directly** to the output terminal with no series capacitor or transformer. This coupling method has been mentioned before, the frequency response being far better with dc coupling such as this. It does, however, necessitate a split supply, the speaker going to chassis potential. Single supply systems must use an output capacitor, usually the largest component in the entire circuit of a few 1000 μF, with the inevitable frequency distortion. One circuit can be converted to the other if desired but plan this carefully. The circuit in figure 4.1 will drive a loudspeaker or headphones acting as a simple beginner's amplifier (construction details in figure 4.20).

A class A amplifier feeding a 35 Ω speaker is shown in figure 4.2, connected as an **intercom**. The 2N3053 is the small version of the 2N3055, supplying 1 W of output in this case. The input stage will also accept a 35 Ω input so that the intercom speaker can be used as a microphone as well. AC coupling is used between all stages but frequency response is not of utmost importance in this circuit. One speaker can be at a distance from **master control** — used as a **baby alarm**, the sweet sound of the yelling baby is heard in the receive position so in the send position you can shout back!

The circuit in figure 4.3 raises the power to 10 W by adding a BD131 driver transistor and a BC158 preamplifier. A single supply rail is used so a 2200 μF coupling capacitor feeds the loudspeaker — the larger the better. This circuit also incorporates the following useful design features.

(1) **Temperature stabilisation** to prevent the biasing of the output transistors drifting with **temperature** rise. The BC108 transistor acts like the two diodes in figure 4.1 but this time their characteristics can change with temperature to offset any temperature change; sometimes a thermistor is used instead.

(2) **Output transistor bias adjustment**. The BC108 bias is adjustable via the 100 Ω resistor to compensate for any unbalance in the output stage, adjusted for minimum cross-over distortion.

(3) High frequency **oscillation suppression** in the output stage, caused by the speaker inductance resonating with circuit capacitance to create very high frequency whistles and loss of power. The two 10 Ω circuits suppress these whistles.

(4) **Negative feedback** to flatten the frequency response. The 470 Ω/0.01 μF parallel circuit from output back to the BC158 provides dc feedback to stabilise gain, flatten the response and reduce noise and distortion. Additional feedback is provided by the 22 Ω BC158 resistor which is not decoupled.

(5) Over-all circuit **balance** is achieved with the 47 kΩ preset, adjusted for exactly *half* the supply voltage at the junction of the two 0.47 Ω resistors.

(6) **Supply decoupling** via the 10 kΩ supply feed resistor and 15 μF capacitor to the preamplifier circuit.

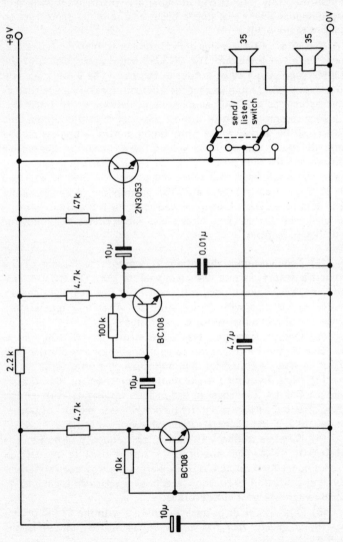

Figure 4.2 Simple intercom using 1 W amplifier

4.2 IC amplifiers

A large number of ICs are available for amplification up to 10 W —
see figures 4.4 to 4.8. Many of these circuits require **heat sinks** since
the operating temperatures must be kept lower than for power transistors. Some circuits have internal or attached heat sinks and it is good
policy to *always* mount power ICs on heat sinks despite the fact that
many include cut-off circuits to protect the IC in case of excessive
temperature.

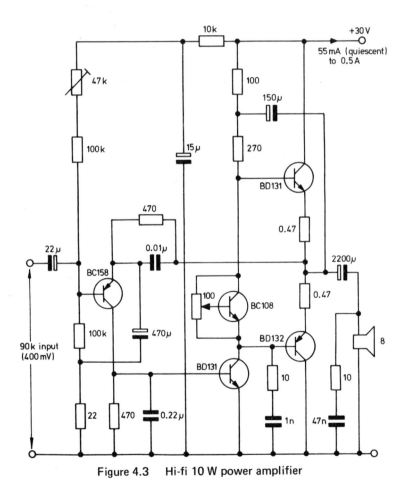

Figure 4.3   Hi-fi 10 W power amplifier

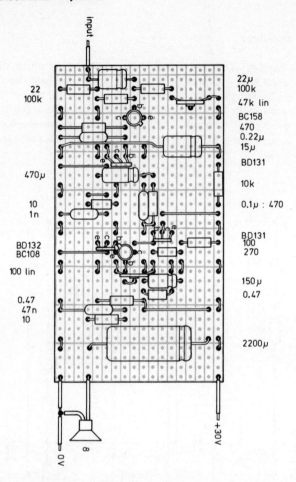

Figure 4.3   (*continued*)

One method used is seen in figure 4.4 where the LM380 2 W amplifier is soldered on to a piece of copper of area about 40 cm^2. The central six pins are designed for this purpose, and the printed circuit board itself can be used as a heat sink. The amplifier shown is intended for a crystal cartridge, volume and simple tone controls being added. The optional 0.047 μF capacitor adds hum rejection to the amplifier at pin 1; ac coupling is used via a 470 μF capacitor to the 8 Ω loudspeaker. Pin 2 need not be connected because this amplifier has the normal differential input like an operational amplifier; an internal resistor is already connected to this point.

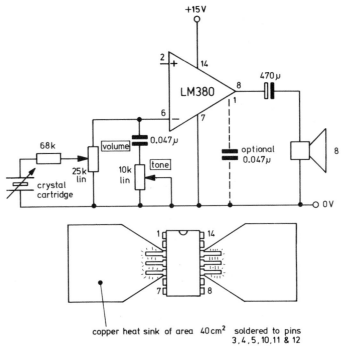

Figure 4.4   LM380 2 W amplifier

An alternative circuit for the LM380 is seen in figure 4.5 where a different type of heat sink is shown. Another optional circuit suppresses high frequency oscillations at the loudspeaker output, as in the transistor circuits. The LM380 is a very versatile and robust amplifier that is highly recommended for a small portable amplifier with minimum complexity — a good start for a beginner with IC amplifiers. Most of the preamplifiers in chapter 3 can be coupled to the LM380 if additional gain is necessary, or better tone correction.

Stereo operation uses either two LM380 circuits for the two channels or a single LM377 which is a 2 + 2 W IC (see figure 4.6). The LM377 again has differential inputs and a single supply rail, driving a 8 Ω loudspeaker. This circuit also doubles as a useful **headphone** amplifier for mono or stereo, trebles as a **VU meter** amplifier and quadruples as a **peak programme meter**. The peak programme meter circuit is shown with both outputs being rectified and smoothed with bridge rectifiers and electrolytic 4.7 μF capacitors across each output, the dc bias level being indicated on the two meters. The sensitivity of the meters can be adjusted with the 6.8 kΩ

This shows the LM 380 amplifier.   The prototype used a socket for mounting the circuit, but better heat dissipation is obtained if the IC is soldered directly to the Veroboard.

resistor; a VU meter is formed by removing the 4.7 µF capacitors to allow the meter to move freely and show **instantaneous signal level**. (The circuit layouts for all circuits are shown in figure 4.21.) The LM377 has a similar heat sink arrangement to the LM380 with 4 W being dissipated via pins 3, 4, 5, 10, 11 and 12.

Two additional IC amplifier circuits giving 4 W and 16 W are shown in figure 4.7. Both circuits require heat sinks and both need to be preceded by a preamplifier to match the pick-up or microphone. The LM379 can be used either as two individual 8 W amplifiers for stereo or in parallel as shown. *Do not* try this with all power amplifiers although two such examples are given in this book. The input impedance of the LM379 is 3 MΩ and the IC has internal current limiting, thermal protection, 0.07 per cent distortion and 70 dB channel separation.

A 21 Watt IC amplifier is shown in figure 4.8 using the TDA 2030 to form a very compact but powerful amplifier with 0.1 per cent distortion and very low noise level. The supply voltage can be ±6 V to ±18 V or the amplifier can be run from a single supply rail. The

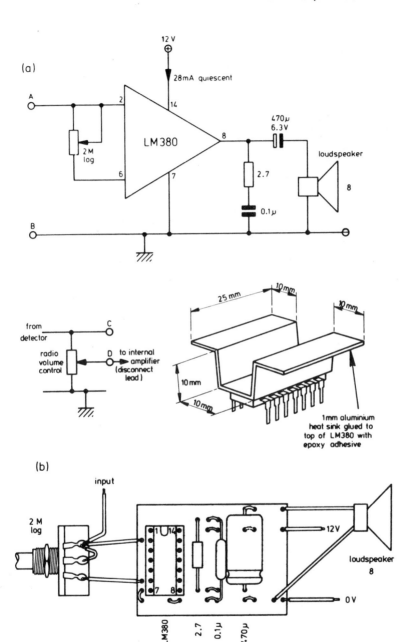

Figure 4.5   Alternative LM380 amplifier

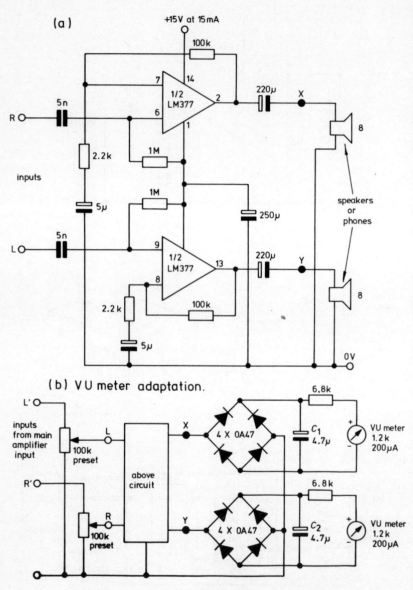

(a)

(b) VU meter adaptation.

Figure 4.6   Simple stereo LM377 2 + 2 amplifier

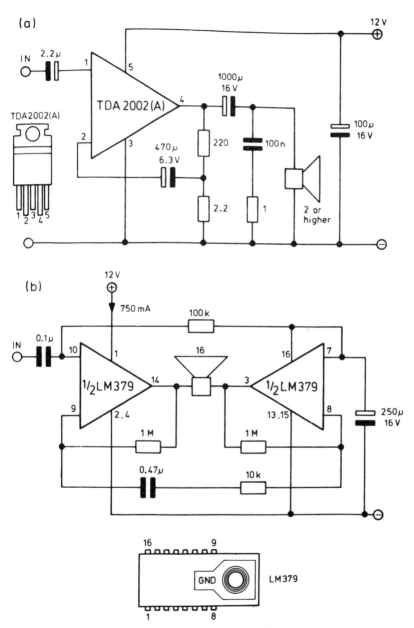

Figure 4.7   IC audio amplifiers

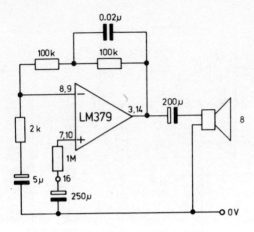

Figure 4.7   (*continued*)

single supply needs the normal large 1000 μF output capacitor in
series with the speaker, using the modified circuit as shown with the
input to pin 1 being changed. The output power will be lower if the
supply voltage is lower or if the loudspeaker impedance is higher.
This also requires a preamplifier and volume control for most
applications and a heat sink 100 mm x 70 mm bolted to the metal
case.

For powers higher than 20 W, ICs become difficult to design
because of the excessive heat dissipation from such a small area. The
normal practice is to use an IC as preamplifier and driver stage with
transistors as the power output. A combination such as this can be
found in some excellent **hybrid** amplifiers such as the HY50 seen in
figure 4.9. These are plastics encapsulated modules with their own
integral heat sink and come in the following sizes

HY50	25 W into 8 Ω
HY120	60 W into 8 Ω
HY200	120 W into 8 Ω
HY400	240 W into 4 Ω

(Now don't rush out and buy a HY400 stereo unit for your living
room — it needs 240 W loudspeakers and about 15 A of supply!)
These amplifiers are almost indestructible with protection of all
kinds for short-circuits, open-circuits, thermal overload, etc. They
are low priced, easily available with low distortion of 0.04 per cent

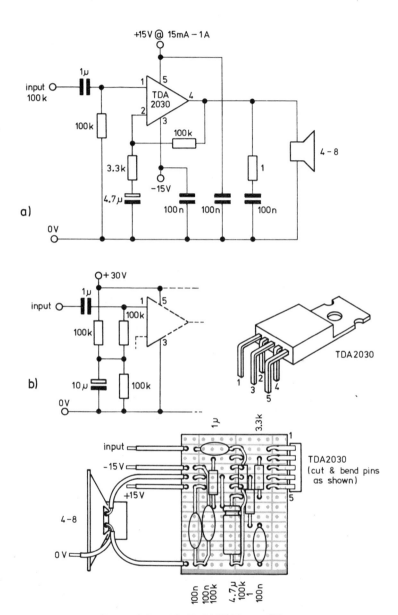

Figure 4.8   90 dB 21 W IC amplifier

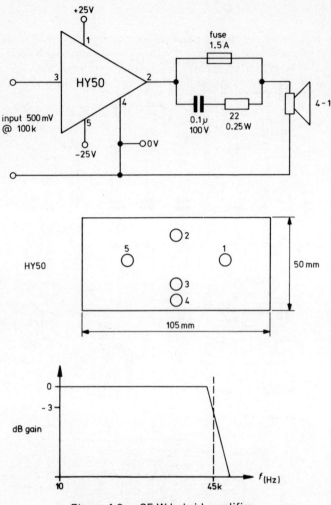

Figure 4.9   25 W hybrid amplifier

at 25 W, 75 dB signal-to-noise ratio and 100 kΩ 500 mV input. They must run from a split power supply and the circuit uses a minimum of components. Power supply units can be purchased but one such as that shown in figure 4.13 is adequate. These hybrid circuits are primarily designed for the HY5 preamplifier of chapter 3 but any preamplifier with 500 mV output will do.

4.3 IC and Transistor Amplifiers up to 100 W

The first power circuit uses a complementary *npn–pnp* output stage using two 2N3055 transistors. One of these is the *pnp* version (a special for push–pull outputs) and the other the normal *npn* version. These are driven by two smaller transistors, the BC182 and BC212

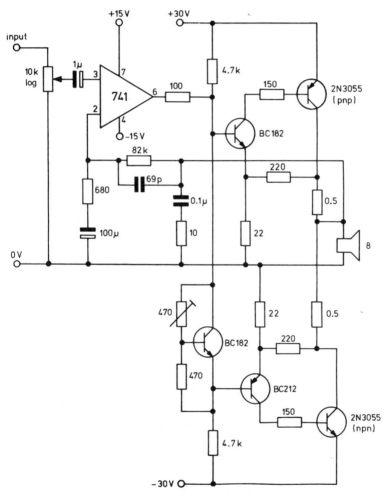

Figure 4.10   40 dB 20 W amplifier

which are biased by a second BC182 (as in figure 4.3), with bias adjustment provided by a 470 Ω preset. A 741 provides preamplification with negative feedback applied between the loudspeaker and the 741 input using a frequency selective circuit. A split supply is used to eliminate the output capacitor; this circuit produces, with a preamplifier of chapter 3, a very pleasing little hi-fi amplifier. The constructional details are shown in figure 4.21 which mounts the output transistors on the printed panel. The heat dissipation must be watched, however, and these 2N3055s must be spaced a few millimeters above the board as shown to allow cooling air to circulate round them. If a metal chassis is used it is better to mount the 2N3055s on to the chassis using mica washers for insulation.

A more powerful amplifier is seen in figure 4.11, with construction details in figure 4.22. Three dc coupled transistors supply the output power in each half — this type of connection is called the **Darlington pair**. The input BC107/BC177 transistors form a dc coupled voltage amplifier, R_1 and the two diodes determine the dc levels throughout the amplifier. Resistors R_2 and R_3 bias the output transistors to their cut-off points so that they *just* turn on when the signal rises above or falls below zero potential. The components connected to the emitter of the input BC107 stabilise the gain which is very high. The input sensitivity is 400 mV, R_4 being adjusted to suit the input; this also ensures low hum levels and the negative feedback uses R_4 and R_5 to give low noise and distortion figures.

This amplifier can be modified for a wide range of output powers as shown in table 4.1; the speaker impedance, supply rail and R are adjusted accordingly. The layout is seen in figure 4.22, again with the output transistors mounted either on the board up to 20 W or on metal heat sinks above 20 W.

One circuit that uses an IC as input and driver amplifier, the LM391, is shown in figure 4.12. The output transistors are similar in configuration to those already described but with the biasing circuits *inside* the LM391. 1 V of signal is required at the input, all necessary equalisation being included in the LM391. Two of these circuits are needed for 100 W output, connected as shown in figure 4.13, an 8 Ω loudspeaker being used (100 W of course). The speaker is connected between point 'X' on one circuit and point 'X' on the second circuit, a suitable split power supply being used with suggested circuit in figure 4.13. The transformer and diodes should be any suitable ones capable of supplying 4 A. The output capacitance of each rail is 9400 μF and two 6.3 A fuses are included for protection of the circuit and power supply under fault conditions.

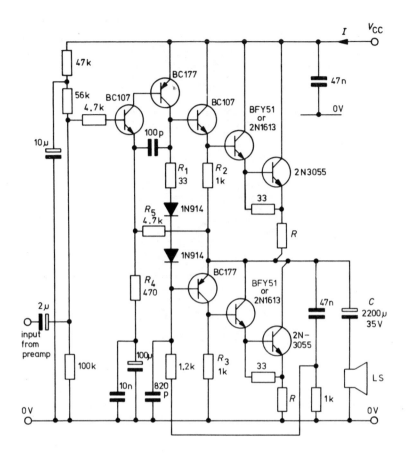

output power (W)	V_{CC} (V)	I (A)	LS (Ω)	R (1W) (Ω)	C and voltage
9	30	1	8	0.22	2200μ 25V
20	30	2	4	0.22	4700μ 25V
40	42	2.5	4	0.22	4700μ 35V
70	42	5	2	0.10	10000μ 35V

Figure 4.11   9/20/40/70 W amplifier

This shows the power amplifier. The transistors must be mounted with insulating washers, and the heat sink mounted where air can circulate round it, preferably vertically. The wires between the output transistors and the circuit board should be kept as short as possible.

4.3.1 Measurement of Amplifier Output Power

Hi-fi enthusiasts and constructors often want to measure the **output power** of their system. A very simple measurement allows this to be done using the relationship power = $I^2 R$ W or V^2/R W. Since ac current is difficult to measure, the ac voltage is measured using a multimeter across the loudspeaker. The output voltage is measured for a constant tone and the measured voltage (rms value) is substituted into V^2/R W, R being the impedance of the loudspeaker whose equivalent resistance is assumed to equal its input impedance. More complex and accurate methods are possible but these involve

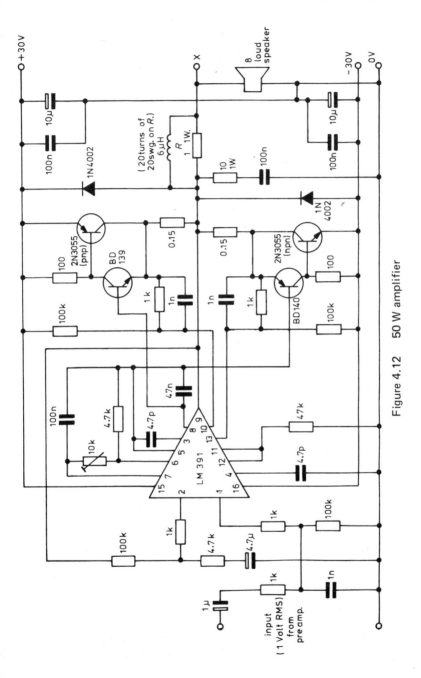

Figure 4.12   50 W amplifier

(a)

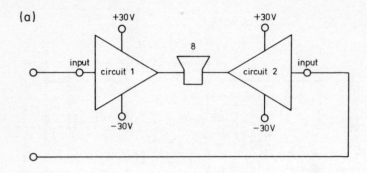

(b)

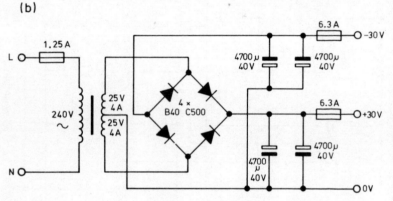

Figure 4.13   (a) push-pull 100 W amplifier, (b) a suitable power supply

the inclusion of dummy loads through which the current and voltage flow are measured.

4.4 Loudspeaker Cross-over Units and Circuits

The most important part of the hi-fi set is the **loudspeaker** and in this section a few simple loudspeaker circuits are described which will improve the over-all sound or add colour to the audio output. Chapter 1 described the need for routing the bass, middle and treble sounds to bass, middle and treble speakers. Two such systems are shown in figure 4.14 where two **passive** networks are shown together with their frequency responses. These circuits form **low** and **high pass filters** through which high level ac signals flow. Thus the capacitors

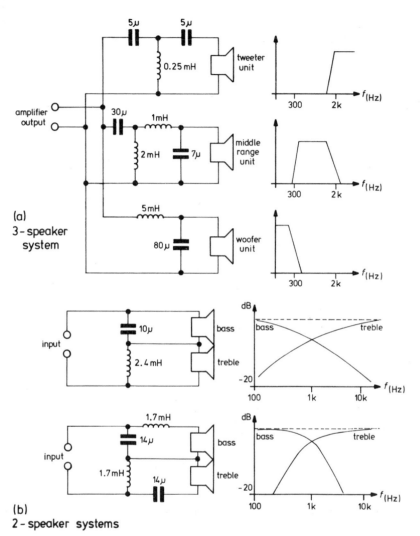

Figure 4.14   Passive loudspeaker cross-over units

used should *not* be electrolytic but should be **non-polarised** types such as **paper** capacitors. The inductors also should be capable of passing the current — many suppliers stock these popular values for this purpose. Figure 4.14b shows two circuits with different filter responses, one being more critical than the other for better separation of treble and bass.

A second system, shown in figure 4.15, uses **active** filters to separate the bass and treble sounds, each loudspeaker having its own power amplifier driven by either a low or high pass filter amplifier as shown. The treble circuit simply filters out all except the treble in the transistor emitter circuit. The bass circuit uses more amplification and incorporates negative feedback to give a flat bass response to this loudspeaker. The 1 Ω resistor and 1 kΩ preset set the gain of this amplifier — too much gain gives a boomy sound. The other presets are adjusted for good balance between the bass and treble outputs.

Quadraphony has arrived and any of the amplifiers shown can be used as the four amplifiers needed in such a system. If, like me, you cannot afford a full quadra system, then try a **pseudo-quad** system such as that shown in figure 4.16. The simple three-speaker system is not really quadra but **treblo** or **triophony** since it adds only one additional speaker behind the listener. This third speaker transmits the **left—right** signal which gives a **background** sound to the stereo, sometimes called **ambience.** This speaker can be of *any* size and, if its output needs to be boosted then small wire-wound resistors can be placed in the earth leads of the two left and right speakers. A ganged wirewound 50 Ω potentiometer would provide some form of adjustment.

Figure 4.16b shows a more comprehensive circuit, the **Hafler** circuit, using four speakers. This system splits the ambience into left and right, with the amount of quadra being adjusted with R_1, R_2 and R_3. Greater volume can again be introduced with the ganged wirewound 50 Ω potentiometer placed in the two earth leads, remembering that this control must pass the main output power of several W, and therefore several amperes.

4.5 Testing Hi-fi Systems

If you have access to an audio signal generator and oscilloscope, you can easily test your audio system by injecting a 1 kHz squarewave into the inputs and observing the waveform at the loudspeaker output. The squarewave, as seen in figure 4.17, can be seen to be made up of an *infinite* number of **odd harmonics** of the fundamental, all added together in different proportions. Observation of the output shows which of these harmonics have been filtered out by possible errors in the amplifier.

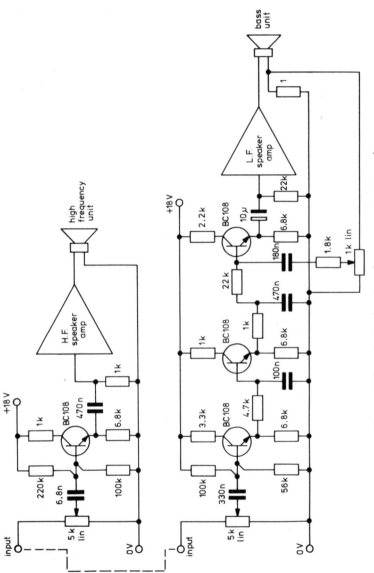

Figure 4.15   Active loudspeaker cross-over network

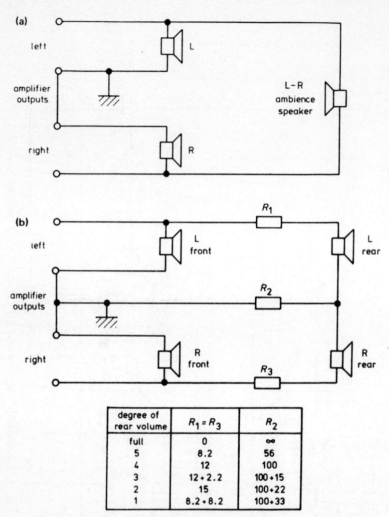

degree of rear volume	$R_1 = R_3$	R_2
full	0	∞
5	8.2	56
4	12	100
3	12 + 2.2	100 + 15
2	15	100 + 22
1	8.2 + 8.2	100 + 33

Figure 4.16   Pseudo-quad

The various controls should first be set for a **flat** frequency response and the input squarewave amplitude adjusted until clipping does *not* take place. The shape of the output signal is observed and then compared with the examples shown in the diagram, any errors being identified as shown. It is good practice to check that the **input** waveform is square as well — if not, then you have problems with your equipment.

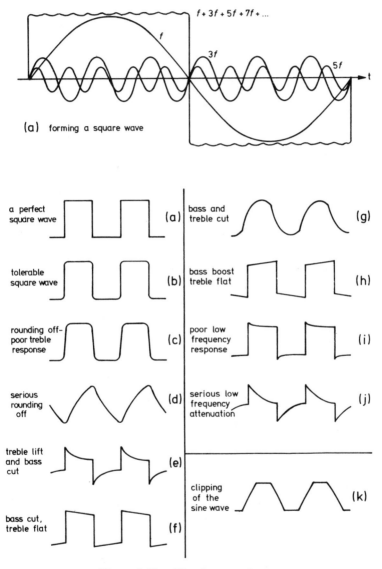

Figure 4.17   Waveform-testing

The waveforms are distorted by the integrating and differentiating of the squarewave, the worst case of distortion being a pure sinewave output. In this case the amplifier is behaving as a perfect filter at the injected frequency of 1 kHz. The waveform in figure 4.17k shows clipping caused either by too much input or by unbalance of the output transistors. Adjustment of the bias preset of figure 4.3 should eliminate this unbalance. (A sinewave input is assumed here.)

4.5.1 Performance Figures

A large number of figures are quoted by hi-fi manufacturers who attempt to baffle the public with misleading statistics. The following is a guide to both commercial and do-it-yourself amplifiers.

(1) **Power output**. This figure is not of great importance since the listener cannot distinguish between, say, 20 and 25 W. The approximate figure is adequate with **r.m.s. watts** into an 8 Ω speaker being quoted when the amplifier is being fed with a 1 kHz tone to produce 1 per cent distortion. Some manufacturers delight in quoting **peak** power or **music** power or power into other impedance outputs since the larger power figures are more impressive — *ignore them*.

(2) **Power bandwidth**. This is not usually a problem with most systems being capable of adequate power output between the 3 dB points with reference to 0 dB at 1 kHz.

(3) **Tone burst**. This test involves the ability of the amplifier to cope with music bursts of, say, a crash of cymbals.

(4) **Damping**. Too much damping will lower the low frequency response since the cone cannot move freely. The output sounds rather muffled and a factor of 10 or more at 25 Hz is satisfactory.

(5) **Cross-over distortion**. This must not be confused with cross-talk. True cross-over distortion, from figure 4.1, is the inability of the two output transistors to work together. The output sounds distorted and seldom presents trouble in new equipment.

(6) **Cross-talk**. This is the breakthrough between left and right channels of a stereo system, or between the four channels of a quadra system. It is tested by injecting a full signal into one channel and detecting any output from the quiet channel — a figure of 66 dB or higher is expected.

(7) **Transient response**. This is the second type of distortion which subjects the amplifier to a sudden jump in input to full power. A number of amplifiers cannot cope with this and either blow the fuses or produce harmonic distortion (a rasping noise) as a result.

(8) **Frequency response**. This identifies the low and high

frequency limits of the entire system, 10 Hz and 50 kHz being preferred as the two limits for true hi-fi.

(9) **Tone control** and **equalisation**. Chapter 3 described the requirement for RIAA equalisation and at least ±10 dB correction at bass and treble frequencies to suit the listener. The mid-positions of each control should produce a perfectly flat response around 1 kHz. Filters should be included for tape hiss and other input errors and they should be sharp enough so as not to affect the nearby frequencies. The **turnover** frequency is that frequency when the filter level has fallen by a half, the **slope** is the rate of fall of the filter response. The turnover figure should be close to the filter frequency and the slope should be high.

(10) **Signal-to-noise ratio**. This covers noise and hum; the figures are measured in **CCIR weighted** dBs which relates all dB measurements to a zero reference level corresponding to zero noise level. Remember that discs and tapes introduce their own noise into the system but the amplifier should not introduce any more noise — you are looking for figures of 63 dB or higher.

(11) **Inputs and outputs**. The **sensitivities** of the inputs and impedances of inputs and output are essential for matching. **Overload** figures at each input are useful as are the alternative outputs to headphones and tape recorders. One final test to be performed involves the simple switching on and off of the amplifier. If a loud thump is heard on the loudspeaker, this should be suppressed so that the loudspeaker is not damaged. A mains capacitor placed across the mains switch contacts should correct this. Protection of each loudspeaker or amplifier by separate fuses to each speaker is recommended, values of 1 to 2 A will be suitable.

4.6 Power Supplies

Three kinds of power supply are shown in figures 4.18 and 4.19. The first delivers 0.5 A via either a fixed voltage output or a variable output (figures 4.18a and b respectively). A 741 is used as an **error amplifier** to control the series regulator transistor BFY51 or AD161. The BFY51 output can be adjusted slightly via the 5 kΩ preset, the AD161 output is continuously variable via the 20 kΩ potentiometer for a small bench power supply for any small amplifier circuit. The AD161 can be replaced by a BD131 if desired, the silicon transistor being more robust and less temperature sensitive.

If greater current is required, the circuits of figure 4.19 can be used — both are **power series regulators** using similar designs. The

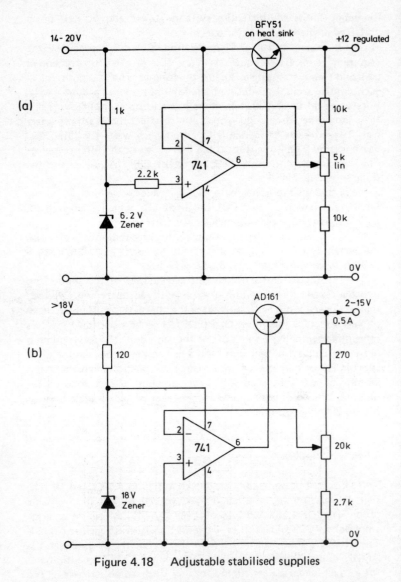

Figure 4.18   Adjustable stabilised supplies

transformer and diodes should be capable of delivering the appropriate current, the 2N3055 being mounted on a suitable heat sink (separate, or the metal chassis). Construction details are given in figure 4.23. A small preamplifier output is included in figure 4.19b which can be added to any power supply circuit such as this where

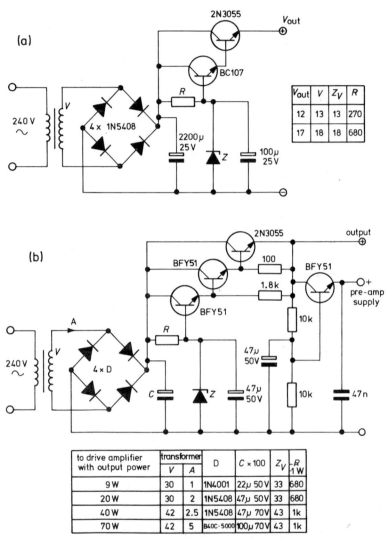

V_{out}	V	Z_V	R
12	13	13	270
17	18	18	680

to drive amplifier with output power	transformer		D	$C \times 100$	Z_V	R ½ W
	V	A				
9 W	30	1	1N4001	22µ 50V	33	680
20 W	30	2	1N5408	47µ 50V	33	680
40 W	42	2.5	1N5408	47µ 70V	43	1k
70 W	42	5	B40C-5000	100µ 70V	43	1k

Figure 4.19   High current power supply

an output resistor chain is provided. One final point concerns power supplies which deliver many amperes (above about 3 A). The copper tracks of printed boards cannot handle this current and so should be reinforced with tinned copper wire (20 swg) which is soldered along the appropriate track (see figure 4.23).

This shows the back view of the power supply. The bridge rectifier diodes should be mounted clear of the board so that air can circulate round them.

This shows the 5 A power supply, viewed from the front. The output sockets should be colour coded, and preferably of dissimilar diameter to prevent incorrect connection.

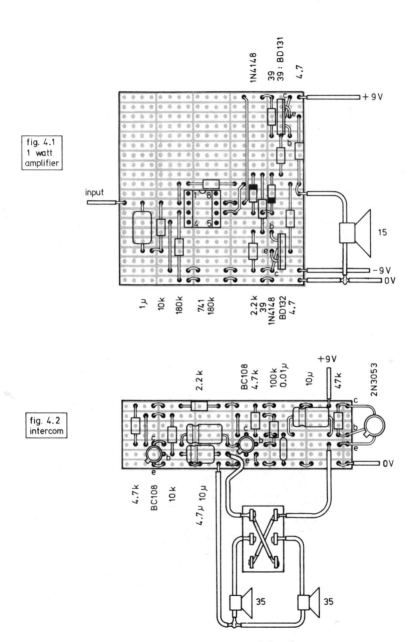

Figure 4.20   Constructional details

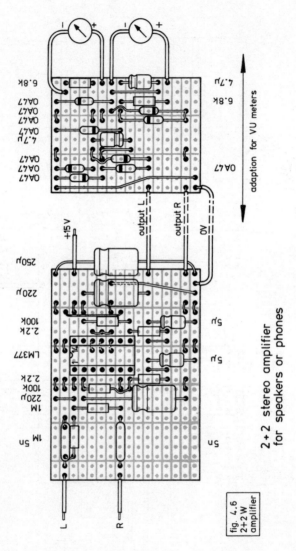

Figure 4.21   Constructional details

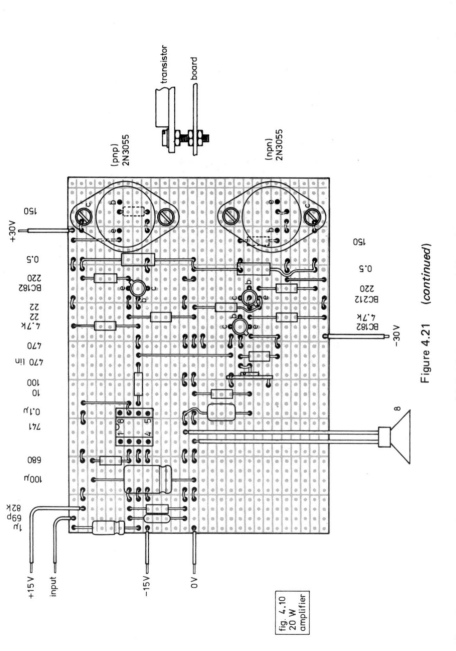

Figure 4.21 (continued)

fig. 4.10
20 W
amplifier

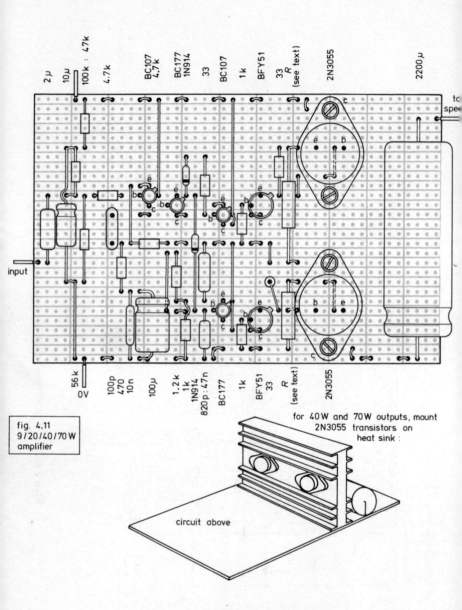

2 μ
10 μ
100k : 47k
4.7k
BC107
4.7k
BC177
1N914
33
BC107
1k
BFY51
33
R
(see text)
2N3055
2200 μ

input

to
speaker

56 k
0V
100p
470
10n
100μ
1.2 k
1k
1N914
820p : 47n
BC177
1k
BFY51
33
R
(see text)
2N3055

fig. 4.11
9 / 20 / 40 / 70 W
amplifier

for 40 W and 70 W outputs, mount
2N3055 transistors on
heat sink :

circuit above

Figure 4.22   Constructional details

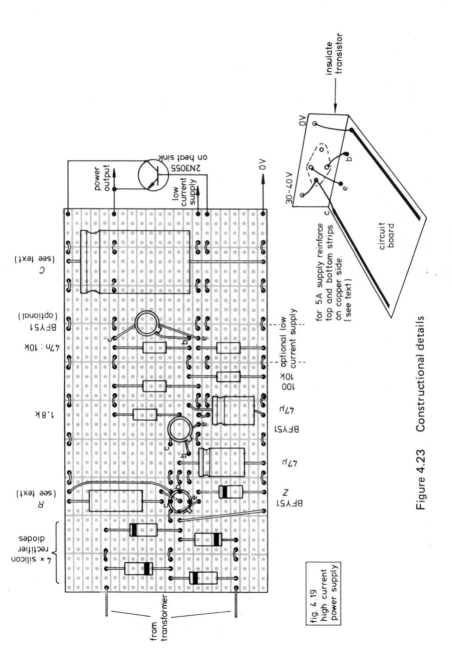

Figure 4.23   Constructional details

5
Noise and Rhythm Circuits

Audio circuits are not merely confined to amplifiers and preamplifiers, they can also make noises and other interesting sounds. They produce **rhythm** sounds for organs and musicians, they produce **phasing** sounds and fuzz noises and a multitude of other experimental noises. For example, flies can be kept out of the kitchen by a 25 kHz oscillator formed from a simple oscillator and crystal earpiece — this is the mating frequency of the fly which sends the females flying. Theatrical groups often need the sounds of the sea, the wind, or 'outer space' (the circuits given in this chapter will produce them), the talking piano or those awful high pitched singer sounds. Electronic synthesisers consist of very many of these circuits all interconnected by a small patch panel connecting the various inputs and outputs. You can quite easily build such a unit, taking each circuit in this chapter and chapter 7 as a small module or building block of the larger system. Try to adopt a similar power supply rail in each case and use the preamplifier and amplifier circuits of the previous chapters for power output.

5.1 Waveform Generation

The basic module of any synthesiser is the **tone generator**. The output of this module can be a sinewave or squarewave, but a square-wave is more versatile since it can be filtered to produce a variety of other waveshapes and sounds. The frequency and amplitude of this generator can be altered and a simple keyboard is constructed to produce the musical sounds of the piano or organ. Figure 5.1 shows

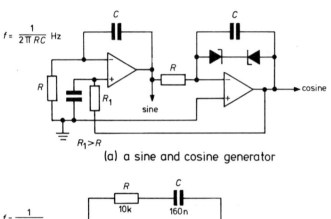

$$f = \frac{1}{2\pi RC} \text{ Hz}$$

$R_1 > R$

(a) a sine and cosine generator

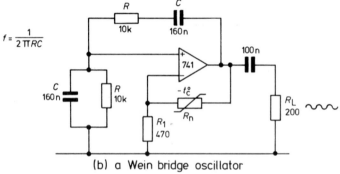

$$f = \frac{1}{2\pi RC}$$

(b) a Wein bridge oscillator

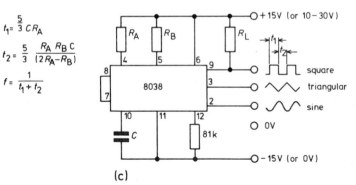

$$t_1 = \frac{5}{3} C R_A$$

$$t_2 = \frac{5}{3} \frac{R_A R_B C}{(2 R_A - R_B)}$$

$$f = \frac{1}{t_1 + t_2}$$

(c)

Figure 5.1 Waveform generators

a simple 741 sine generator in two forms, one being a twin 741 **integrator** circuit and the other a **Wien bridge** sinewave oscillator. The frequency of each can be adjusted as shown so that the constructor can vary the output; both circuits need ganged resistors to vary the frequency.

The circuit in figure 5.1c uses the popular 8038 IC to generate square, sine or triangular outputs over a wide range of frequencies. The mark—space ratio can be altered (t_1/t_2) to produce pulses or distorted sinewaves or sawtooth waves; each has its characteristic sound. This IC is a worthwhile investment for a synthesiser, with variable or fixed outputs. It is interesting to note that this IC generates the sinewave by very complex circuitry — the sinewave is split into a large number of portions and added together at the output. The errors are almost undetectable on an oscilloscope.

5.2 Attack and Decay Circuits

A musical instrument *sounds* like a musical instrument because of the amount of **attack** and **decay** of the sound. A pure sinewave can be made to sound like a flute by adding the appropriate attack to the sound. If attack and decay are added a piano sound is formed. The circuits in this section can shape *any* waveform into any other to produce a variety of sounds. A simple circuit is shown in figure 5.2 (with more in figures 5.3c and 5.4b). This converts a steady tone into a musical note, the tone being generated internally, in this case, by a simple **multivibrator** formed by two cross-coupled transistors. (Electronics magazines are flooded by 1001-purpose multivibrator circuits.) It is used here as yet another source of squarewaves with *npn* transistors in figure 5.2 and *pnp* transistors in figure 5.3a — either will do. The squarewave is altered in amplitude by the attack/ decay circuit involving TR1 to TR4. TR1 and TR4 are placed across the oscillator signal, each transistor acting like a variable resistor in parallel, with the signal.

When switch S is in its *on* position as shown, TR1 and TR4 are both conducting to short the squarewave to chassis. As S is opened TR2 turns *on* which, after C_1 has charged up via R_1, turns *off* TR1. At the same time TR3 turns *on* to discharge the 10 μF capacitor, TR4 also being turned *off*. This capacitor now charges up and the output squarewave decays to zero in a short time. Attack and decay times can be adjusted, as can the multivibrator to provide different output tones.

A simple comprehensive rhythm generator is seen in figure 5.3

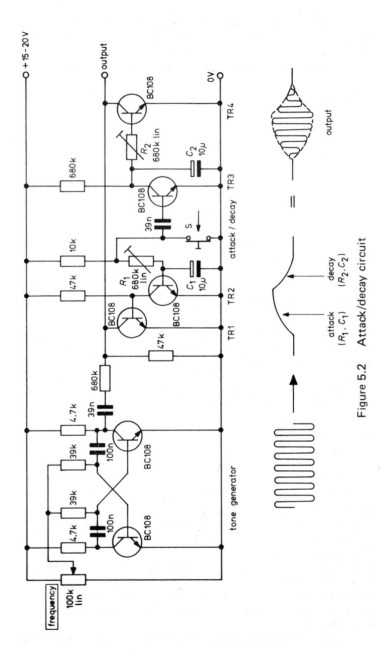

Figure 5.2 Attack/decay circuit

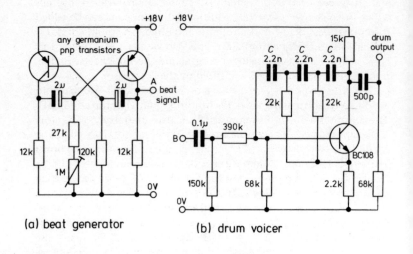

(a) beat generator

(b) drum voicer

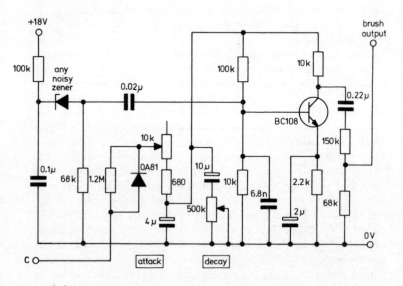

(c) brush / cymbals circuit

Figure 5.3   Rhythm generator modules

with a multivibrator beat generator which feeds both drum circuit and brush/cymbals circuits. Points A, B and C are connected together either directly or via switches; additional drum circuits can be added for bongo, bass or other drum noises if desired. The multivibrator is similar to figure 5.2; adjustment is provided via the 1 MΩ preset, this being a low frequency oscillator to generate the slow beats. Reduction of the capacitor values will speed up the beats.

The drum voicer is a three-stage oscillator which is brought into action by the input trigger pulse from the multivibrator at point B. The output is a burst of sinewaves of the drum frequency, capacitors C being adjusted for the appropriate drum noise. The circuit in figure 5.3c is a further attack and decay circuit for producing **brush** and **cymbals** sounds. A **noisy Zener** diode is chosen — these can be bought for this purpose or any top-hat variety of Zener can be tried in this position to generate 100 mV of noise. The 4 μF capacitor charges via the 68 Ω resistor and 10 kΩ preset for attack; the 10 μF capacitor charges via the 500 kΩ preset for decay. The input pulse is therefore shaped to turn *on* the BC108 noise amplifier, the pulse serving as the supply voltage for this brief period. The components for this circuit, as in many other synthesiser circuits, are not critical and experimentation will produce an unlimited variety of sounds.

5.2.1 Synthesisers

A simple synthesiser consists of a **ring modulator**, an **envelope shaping** circuit, a **frequency generator** (both high and low frequency), a **noise generator**, several **filters** at various frequencies or a tunable active filter such as that in chapter 3, a **phasing** circuit and a **patch panel** or set of switches. The circuits of figure 5.4 show the ring modulator circuit and envelope shaper (construction details are given in figure 5.12). The modulator circuit modulates one signal on to another, either signal can take any form whether low or high frequency; the high frequency is normally applied to input 1, the low frequency to input 2. The BC108 **long-tailed-pair** is a balanced circuit found in all differential amplifiers which sends two signals to the mixer BC108, one of which has its amplitude varied by the input 2 signal. The FET is used as a variable resistor to modulate signal 1. Figure 5.4b shows another envelope shaper, this time with a **unijunction** oscillator as the beat generator and simple diode attack and decay circuits. Figures 5.4c and d show two simple applications of these circuits for slow fade up and down of input 1 and voice-operated fading. The second circuit senses a voice input and then uses it to control the fade down of the music signal to input 1. When the voice stops, the music is faded up again making this circuit suitable for disc jockeys.

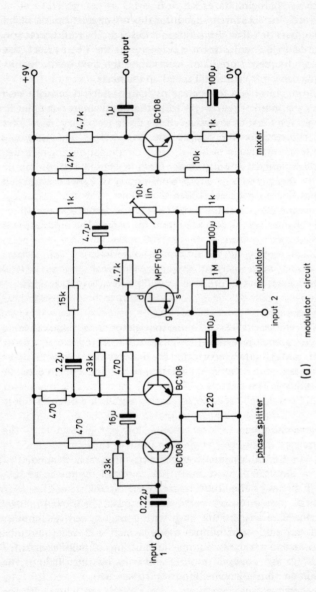

(a) modulator circuit

Figure 5.4 Synthesiser circuits

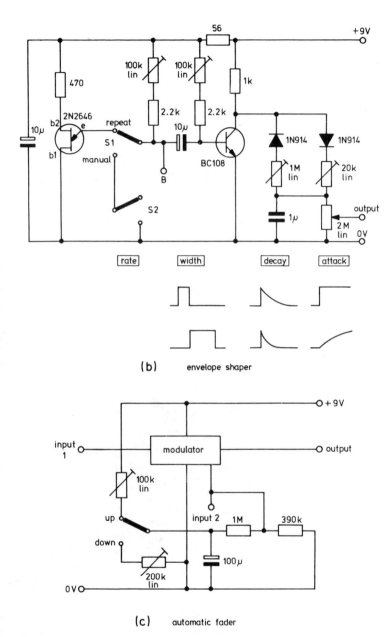

(b)   envelope shaper

(c)   automatic fader

Figure 5.4   (*continued*)

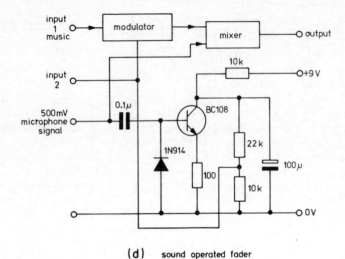

(d) sound operated fader

Figure 5.4 (*continued*)

This shows the completed circuit board for the ring modulator. There is a lot on this relatively small board, so be particularly careful to avoid 'solder bridges'. Take care also that the component leads do not short against each other.

If the two inputs are connected together by a 0.1 μF capacitor, a frequency doubling circuit is formed with delightful processing of the input music or speech.

5.3 Rhythm Generation

The circuit of figure 5.3 operated as a simple rhythm generator but there was no way of automatically switching the drum and cymbals noises on and off to create different rhythms. A comprehensive rhythm generator creates many dance rhythms and feeds pulses to a variety of drum and cymbal voicing circuits. CMOS technology has provided a pre-programmed ROM circuit (read-only memory) inside which the various rhythms are created through a matrix of diodes and transistors. The M252 is one such circuit, shown in figure 5.5 with a CMOS beat generator driving the M252. The construction is shown in figure 5.13 where you can see how small the unit can be made. These units require +5 V and −12 V; a suitable supply circuit is shown in figure 5.6c with an added +12 V for the 741 circuit of figure 5.6.

The rhythm select switches of the M252 use **binary coding** to select the 15 rhythms and a set of suitable wafer switches or relays is required to produce the 4-digit code for each rhythm. Alternatively digital logic circuits can be used but this makes the unit very complex. A second IC is also available, the M253, which has 16 separate inputs for the rhythm selection but this is larger and more expensive.

The **rhythm voicing** is carried out with a basic drum circuit of figure 5.6a which has C_1, C_2 and C_3 adjusted for the various drum tones. The brush and cymbals circuit of figure 5.6b uses a transistor with open-circuit collector as the source of noise. Various input pulses are applied to the shaping circuits to activate the noise circuit: a snare drum is a combination of drum and brush sounds thereby calling for the snare drum pulse to be fed both to the cymbals circuit as shown and a suitable drum circuit. Similar effects are seen with the maraccas, the cymbals pulses only need be connected as shown. Various drum circuits need to be constructed and parallel connection of these is required at the mixer 741 input; the various controls set the balance between the drum and cymbals sounds (RV_2). RV_1 sets the over-all gain. Full construction details are given in figure 5.13.

5.4 Miscellaneous Signal Processing

Most modern recording studios are full of synthesisers in all shapes

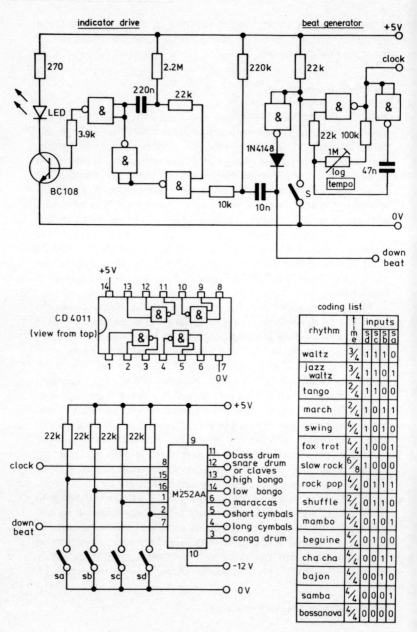

Figure 5.5   IC rhythm generator drive

rhythm	time	inputs			
		sd	sc	sb	sa
waltz	3/4	1	1	1	0
jazz waltz	3/4	1	1	0	1
tango	2/4	1	1	0	0
march	2/4	1	0	1	1
swing	4/4	1	0	1	0
fox trot	4/4	1	0	0	1
slow rock	6/8	1	0	0	0
rock pop	4/4	0	1	1	1
shuffle	2/4	0	1	1	0
mambo	4/4	0	1	0	1
beguine	4/4	0	1	0	0
cha cha	4/4	0	0	1	1
bajon	4/4	0	0	1	0
samba	4/4	0	0	0	1
bossanova	4/4	0	0	0	0

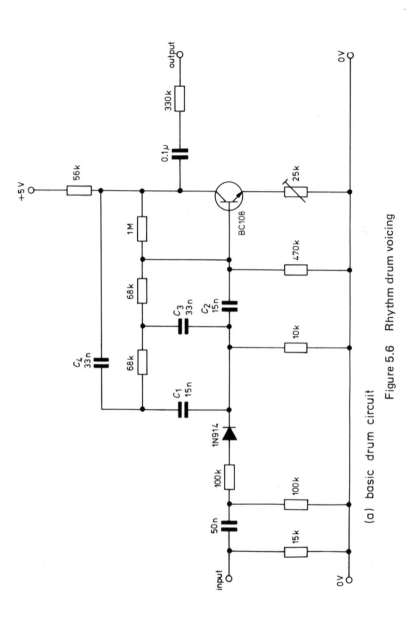

(a) basic drum circuit

Figure 5.6   Rhythm drum voicing

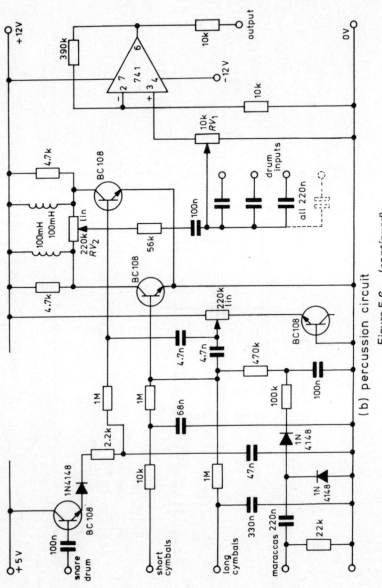

(b) percussion circuit   Figure 5.6   (continued)

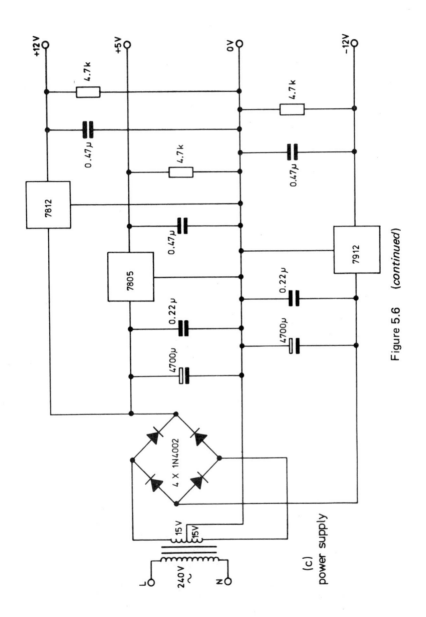

Figure 5.6 *(continued)*

(c) power supply

and forms and all include the circuits given in this section. The first is a **phasing** circuit often called the **waa-waa** circuit because of the sound it makes. The circuit shown in figure 5.7 is an **automatic** phasing circuit which automatically changes the phase of the audio signal as the audio volume rises and falls. The top circuit is an ac bridge circuit whose balance point is set by R_1 and R_2. These resistors can be manually controlled by a dual-ganged 25 kΩ + 25 kΩ potentiometer, or, as shown, with two ORP12 **light dependent resistors**. The ORP12 resistance changes from about 10 kΩ when dark down to a 100 Ω or so when light; these are operated in the shown circuit by two lamp bulbs from the circuit below. As R_1 and R_2 are altered, the bridge goes out of balance to produce the waa-waa effect.

The lower circuit is a simple sound-to-light circuit which amplifies the audio signal and uses it to light the two 6 V bulbs in close proximity to the two ORP12s. This circuit can be added to any hi-fi system to give a most pleasing sound. The circuit includes a form of damping which phases slowly or quickly as switch S is operated. (Constructional details are given in figure 5.14.)

Reverberation can be added to any hi-fi system or synthesiser using the principle shown in figure 5.8. Commercial units are available for this purpose with a metal spring line supported between two magnetic pick-ups. One pick-up is used as the transmitter and the other as the receiver, circuits being included to amplify the signals at both ends. The circuit shown has a 1 W amplifier as the driver and a 741 as receiver-amplifier, a second 741 being used as an output mixer amplifier; the levels are adjusted to suit the listener.

Commercial spring lines are expensive but a good system can be built from two old speakers, preferably small ones as shown. A metal fire element is cut down to about 300 mm and a hook is bent into each end. These hooks are hooked into the centre of each speaker cone, the tension being adjusted so that the line is just stretched by a few centimetres. Do not extend the line too much or the speaker cones will whizz across the room! Listen to the sound and adjust accordingly. (Obviously these speakers will no longer be suitable for normal use.)

True echo is produced in studios in an echo chamber; your bathroom is a good substitute provided you don't run any water while recording! A simpler method of obtaining echo uses a conventional reel-to-reel tape recorder. Some cassette recorders will do but their compact construction makes things difficult. Figure 5.9 shows the method where a normal record amplifier feeds the signal and bias to the record head. A playback head, if not already fitted, is placed a few centimetres from this record head, its output is amplified in a

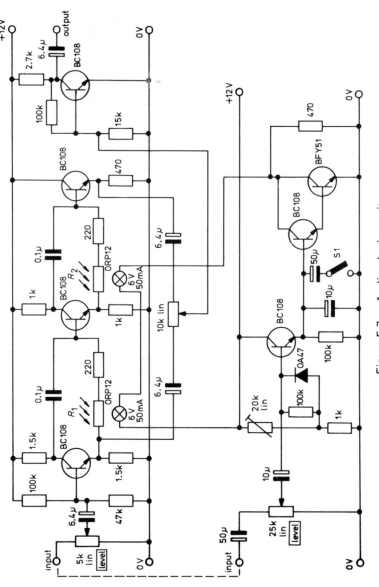

Figure 5.7   Audio phasing unit

This circuit was produced as a prototype phasing unit. The two light-dependent resistors can be seen clearly in the middle of the board, with the bulb soldered in position in between them. Normally this circuit should be sheltered from ambient light for the best operation. This particular board was cut away to enable it to be mounted in a relatively cramped box, along with the controls.

low impedance amplifier (see chapter 3) and this echo is added to the original signal via VR. This same echo is then sent round the circuit again to produce unlimited repeated echos with more playback heads added if necessary. These additional heads can be attenuated if necessary to form the most pleasing effect. The echo distance can be adjusted by either changing the distance d or changing the speed of the tape through the system. An ac mains recorder may not have this facility but a battery or dc motor can be added to allow the motor speed to be changed.

After about an hour or so of echo the tape will run out. This calls for a tape **loop** to be made as shown, but the join must be good otherwise clicks will be heard as the join passes the playback head each time.

Reference was made in chapter 3 to an agc controlled amplifier which maintained a **constant audio output** for a variety of input levels. The two circuits of figure 5.10 use the same MC3340P as before to maintain a constant output. The output signal is amplified in a 741 in figure 5.10a and a BC109 in figure 5.10b; it is rectified

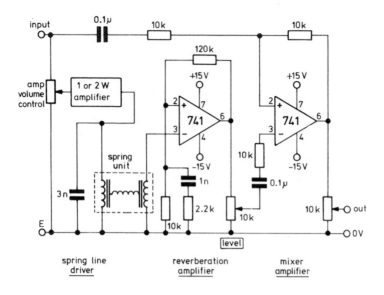

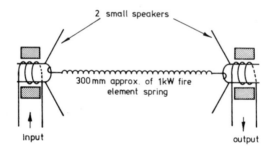

Figure 5.8   Reverberation unit

and smoothed to form a dc bias to be passed to a FET in (a) and a
BC177 in (b) to adjust the gain. These circuits are useful in discos
where the dancers demand a constant output noise, even in quiet
passages of music, despite the fact that the tapes and discs have
already been processed with these compression circuits.

The final circuit, figure 5.11, is a **peak detector indicator** using
another 741. The small LED (light-emitting diode) is mounted on
the front panel and lights up when the signal is overloading the
amplifier. The point at which the LED lights is set by the 100 kΩ

(a)

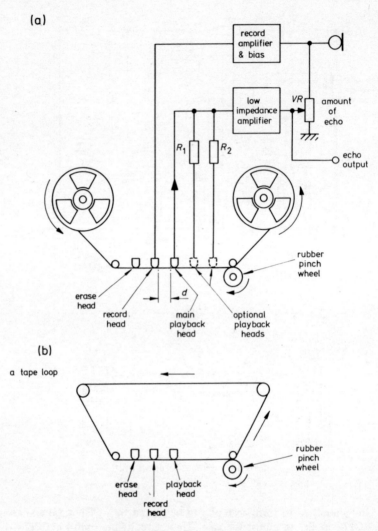

(b)

a tape loop

Figure 5.9 Echo arrangement

control, left and right inputs being fed here to a common indicator although separate circuits can be used for each channel. This circuit is intended primarily for preamplifiers which can easily be overloaded by an excessive input signal. A generator and oscilloscope can be used to set the control if desired, where clipping of the signal will be seen as in figure 4.17k.

(a)

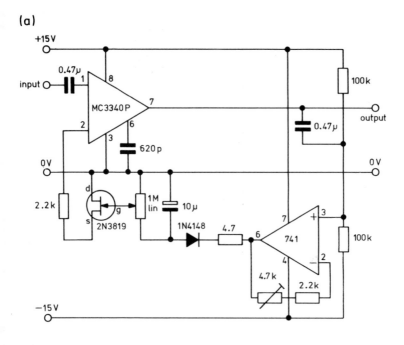

(b)

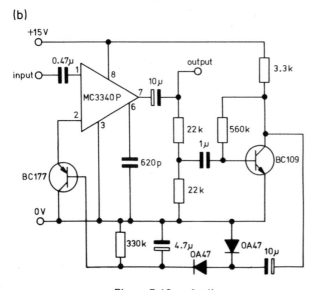

Figure 5.10   Audio compressors

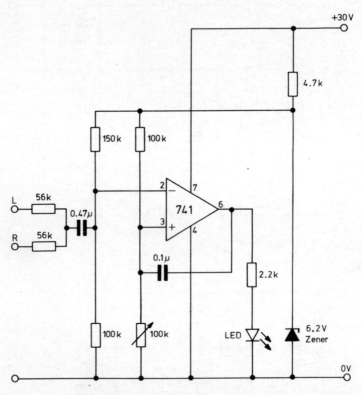

Figure 5.11   Peak overload detector

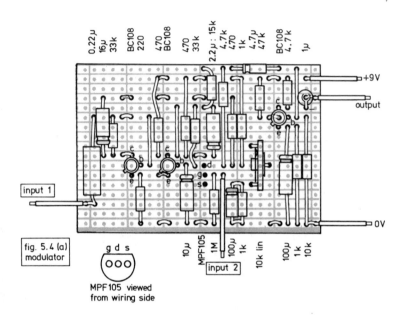

fig. 5.4 (a) modulator

input 1

+9V

output

0V

g d s

MPF105 viewed from wiring side

input 2

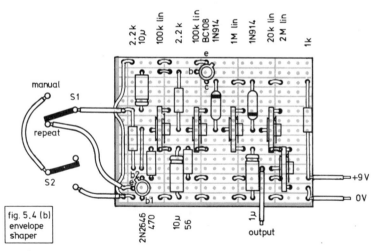

manual

S1

repeat

S2

fig. 5.4 (b) envelope shaper

+9V

0V

output

Figure 5.12   Constructional details

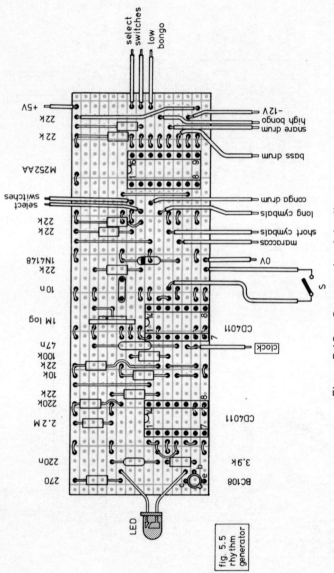

Figure 5.13   Constructional details

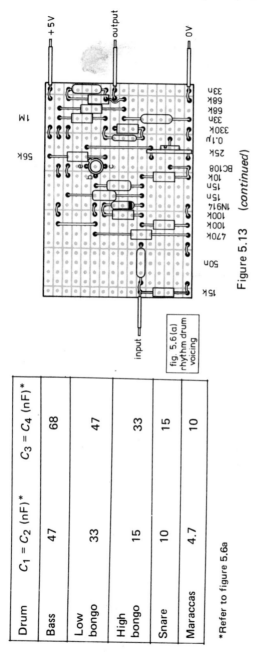

Figure 5.13 (continued)

Drum	$C_1 = C_2$ (nF)*	$C_3 = C_4$ (nF)*
Bass	47	68
Low bongo	33	47
High bongo	15	33
Snare	10	15
Maraccas	4.7	10

*Refer to figure 5.6a

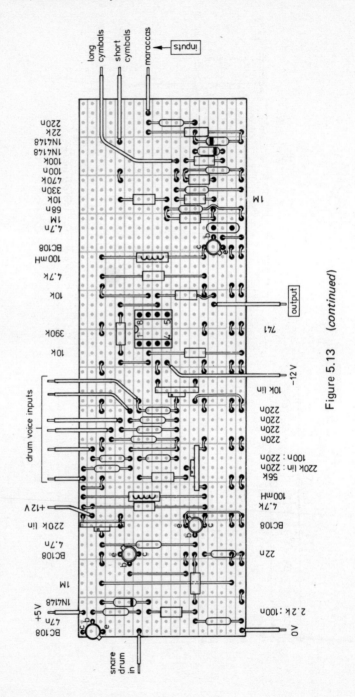

Figure 5.13 *(continued)*

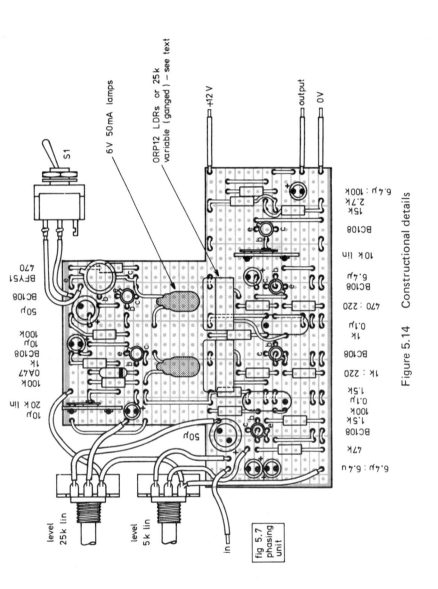

S1

6V 50mA lamps

ORP12 LDRs or 25k
variable (ganged) – see text

+12V

output

0V

6.4µ : 100k
2.7k
15k
BC108

10k lin

6.4µ
BC108
470 : 220

0.1µ
1k
BC108

1k : 220

1.5k
0.1µ
100k
1.5k
BC108

47k

6.4µ : 6.4µ

470
BFY51
BC108

50µ

100k
10µ
BC108
1k
0A47
100k

10µ
20k lin

50µ

level
25k lin

level
5k lin

in

fig 5.7
phasing
unit

Figure 5.14   Constructional details

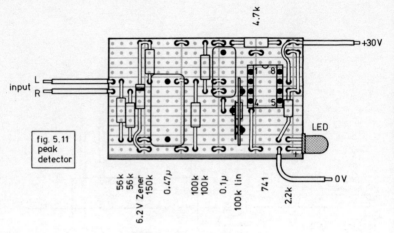

Figure 5.14   (*continued*)

6
Disco Circuits

This chapter shows how the audio signals of the other chapters can be converted into **light** outputs using, for example, coloured lights for discos. The basis of sound-to-light units is the **thyristor** or **triac** which is a power switch that turns on several amperes of ac to an output lamp using a small input voltage to the gate. Once turned on, the thyristor or triac will stay on until its anode voltage falls below that of the cathode. Obviously this creates problems for dc operation, but for ac operation the alternating mains cycle from +300 V to −300 V or so performs this turning off every cycle. Thyristor circuits are well suited to mains operation. The triac is an adaptation of the thyristor which switches on *both* halves of the mains cycle, positive and negative. Thus thyristor switches only on positive halves of the mains producing only half full output brightness on a lamp while the triac produces full output brightness.

One fault associated with thyristors and triacs is the **interference** they transmit due to their high speed switching of high currents. The simple circuits of this chapter cannot prevent this, but a type of switching called a **zero-crossing switch** is used which switches when the current is zero, thereby avoiding the interference output. **Safety** is of the *utmost importance* in all thyristor circuits since mains voltages are everywhere, even on large metal heat sinks. All these circuits ensure **perfect** isolation of the driving circuit from the high voltage thyristor circuit via opto-coupling or pulse transformers. *Never* physically connect the two halves of these circuits together via capacitors or diodes — a tempting operation but *very* dangerous.

6.1 Sound-to-light Circuits

The circuit of figure 5.7 used a simple transistor amplifier to drive two 6 V lamp bulbs and cause them to change brightness with the input music. This circuit, or the circuit of figure 6.1, serves as the **sound-to-light converter**. The ORP12, a light-dependent resistor, detects this light variation and uses it to adjust the timing circuit of the thyristor, causing it to fire at the appropriate point in the mains cycle. If a filter circuit of chapter 3 is used before the sound-to-light circuit, one channel of a **colour organ** is produced. Alternatively a low frequency multivibrator or oscillator can be connected to this circuit to form a simple **stroboscopic** display (figures 5.2 or 5.3 are suitable). Yet another application uses digital logic circuits to generate a sequential string of pulses to turn on and off series of lights in rows or circles. These are called **running lights** and the digital circuit of figure 7.2 is perfectly suitable, the 1N4148 diodes being replaced by LEDs (cathodes earthed) to drive the ORP12s directly to produce a four-channel sequential display. Many lighting effects for discos can be produced with this simple circuit, so *have a go.* Do remember the safety rules and use a good earth on all metal chassis; fuse the mains input in the normal way.

They *cannot*, however, be mounted on to the outside metal chassis since the working voltages are much higher. The heat sinks must therefore be supported with plastics mounts and good air circulation provided. Do not touch these metal heat sinks and do not place them where they can be touched.

Figure 6.1b shows a more complex light modulator which applies the signal to a double-gated low voltage thyristor BRY39A. One gate has a dc supply connected, the other is turned on and off by a small ac signal from TR1. When the thyristor fires, a large pulse is transformed in the pulse transformer (for isolation) to a second thyristor TH2 which is connected to the 500 W load. The thyristor TR2 uses zero-crossing switching from TR1 and so the interference output is small, the timing of the trigger pulses being set by the TR1 gate circuit. A small LED is added for indication on the front panel. The remaining components make up a simple +15 V power supply for driving several of these channels for a colour organ.

(a)

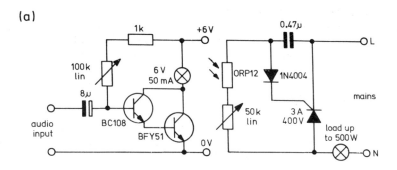

(b)

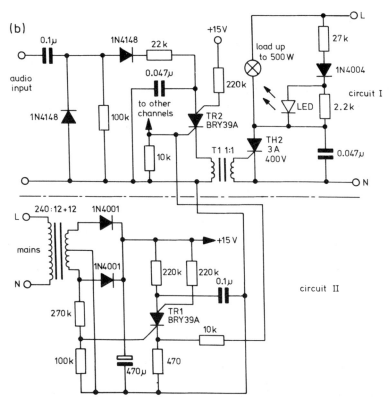

Figure 6.1   Sound-to-light modulators

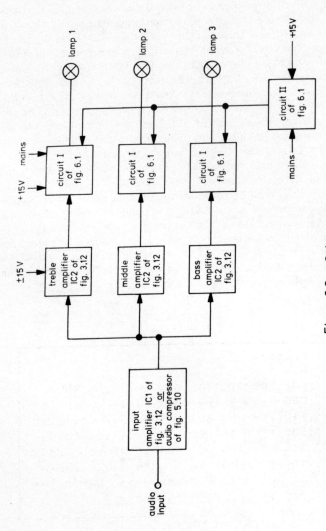

Figure 6.2   Colour organ

6.2 Colour Organs

The amplifier in figure 3.12 or the audio compressor in figure 5.10 provides initial amplification of the audio input and, at the same time, ensures that there is *always* an output from this circuit to supply light to the lamps. In this way the disco hall will never be without light, even in quiet passages. This circuit feeds three tone circuits or filters, one for bass, one for middle and one for treble. The circuit in figure 3.12 will be adequate, the three controls being separated out into **three separate circuits** (see figure 6.2). IC1 remains as the input preamplifier to feed the three 741 filter circuits each using the appropriate part of IC2. The three controls provide bass, middle and treble adjustment, these outputs then each drive circuit I of figure 6.1. All three thyristor circuits are driven by circuit II.

A simpler colour organ circuit is shown in figure 6.3 with construction details in figure 6.4. The input filters are far simpler than before with a simple BC184 driver to each triac circuit via an isolating transformer which is any 2 kΩ : 8 kΩ audio coupling transformer. Perfect isolation between the circuits has to be reinforced with the board of figure 6.4 containing no mains voltages whatsoever. Any 400 V triac can be used, the current rating matching the load. This circuit should be driven from the output of the audio power amplifier, not the preamplifier stage as is the case with figure 6.2.

SAFETY

For safety reasons, two 1µF, 400V capacitors (C_1 and C_2) are used to isolate the audio input. Because of their relatively large size, these are not included on the Veroboard layout shown in figure 6.4. These capacitors must, however, be included as shown in figure 6.3.

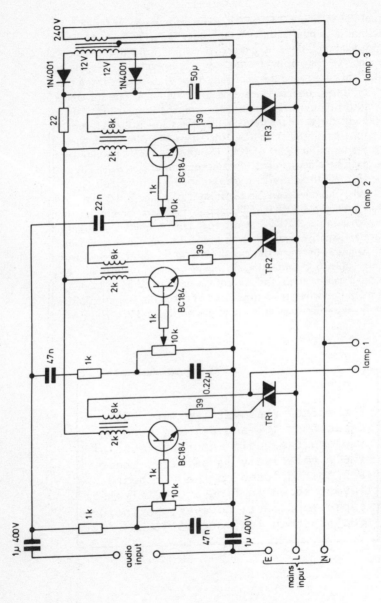

Figure 6.3   Colour organ

note : the BC184 may be supplied with the
base and collector connections interchanged ;
check with supplier

Figure 6.3
colour organ

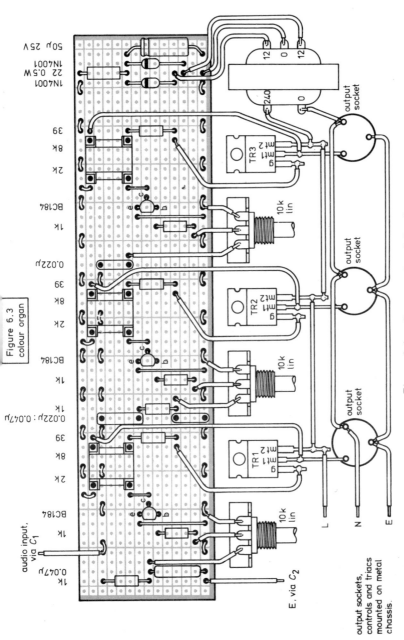

Figure 6.4   Constructional details

7
Music Circuits

The music perfectionist shudders at the thought of electronic music since it does not truly match the original sounds of the musical instrument. Electronic music has a sound of its own and does not always attempt to imitate *exactly* the true instrument. (An electronic instrument does, however, have a volume control and can be used with headphones to avoid annoying the neighbours.) Each circuit can be coupled to any preamplifier or amplifier of earlier chapters, or they can be coupled to the synthesiser circuits of chapter 5 and disco circuits of chapter 6. Some music circuits can be regarded as toys or fun circuits — many an electronic engineer has been introduced to the world of electronics by a gift of such a circuit at an early age.

7.1 Stylophones

The faithful multivibrator is the obvious choice for the generation of electronic music, each note using one of the circuits of figure 5.3a suitably tuned to the correct frequency. Alternatively, one such circuit can be used with individual notes connected by a stylus to a set of variable resistors, one per note taken out to a simple keyboard.

The first system is called **polyphonic** since several notes can be played together. The second circuit is termed **monophonic** since only one note can be played at a time, such as with a brass instrument.

The circuit of figure 7.1a uses a unijunction transistor 2N2646 to generate the tones of the organ and form a **stylophone**. The **stylus**

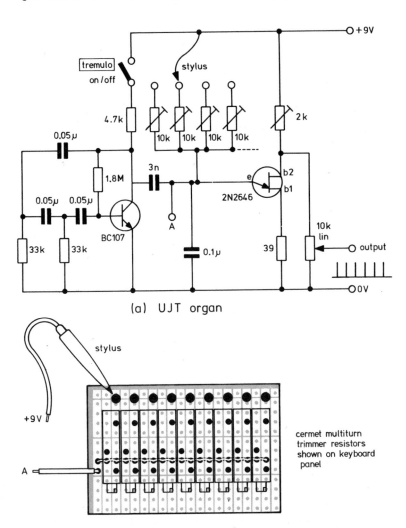

(a) UJT organ

Figure 7.1 Stylophones

(b) 741 alternative oscillator.

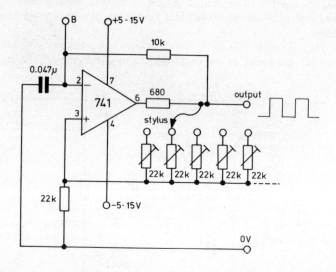

(c) modification for single supply
    for 741

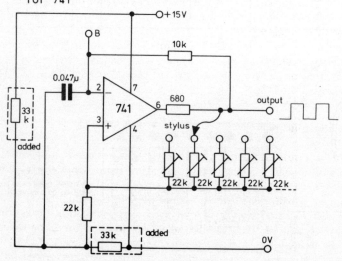

Figure 7.1   (*continued*)

A very simple stylus is shown, the keyboard comprising the copper strips on the underside of the board. The details depend on what you have available!

arrangement is shown — a metal rod or disused ball-point pen with wire soldered to the tip. The variable resistors can be soldered on to the strips of the printed board creating a simple keyboard.

An alternative oscillator uses, of course, a transistor multivibrator or 741 multivibrator which produces an excellent squarewave. The output from one of these oscillators is rather uninteresting and so a **tremulo** is added from a BC107 phase-shift oscillator. The large sinewave output modulates the unijunction output to give the characteristic stylophone sound. Figure 7.1c shows a different 741 multivibrator with single supply rail and two additional 33 kΩ resistors.

7.2 Electronic Music

Circuits have been described which generate a squarewave using multivibrator circuits such as figure 7.2. The output from this circuit drives a BFY51 output transistor and an 8 Ω loudspeaker. The frequency of this oscillator is altered by adjustment of the resistors coupled to each base as before. This digital circuit achieves this *automatically* via the 1N4148 diodes, variable resistors being tuned to the desired frequencies. The notes rotate in sequence 1, 2, 3, 4, 5, 6, 7, 8, 1, 2, and so on indefinitely. The rotation is performed with simple 7495 shift register circuits — these are TTL 5 V circuits

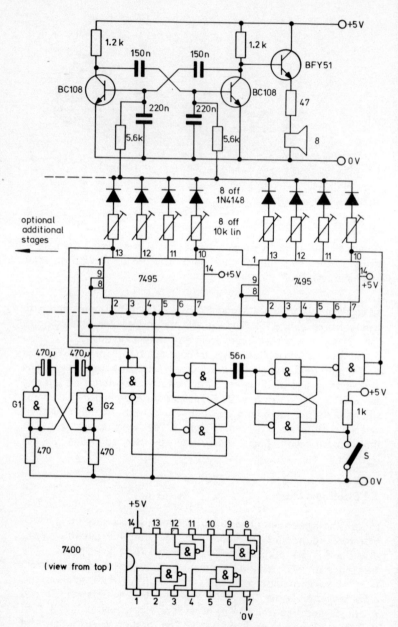

Figure 7.2   Electronic composer

driven by two further TTL 7400 circuits connected as a multivibrator (G1 and G2) and trigger circuit. Switch S stops the circuit when desired and, if used as a door-bell, switch S must be a *normally closed* switch which opens when the push is operated.

Several 7495 circuits can be added to this basic circuit with the wiring following the pattern shown. Only one 5 V supply is needed.

A **polyphonic organ** uses the CMOS technology introduced in chapter 5, namely the AY-1-0212 circuit which incorporates all the necessary divider circuits to change a 1 MHz crystal output into the top octave of an organ. Space does not allow for giving full details of this organ, but the average constructor should be able to complete this project with the details given. A ready wired keyboard is recommended, this contains all the necessary contacts and wiring using ready mounted gold or silver wires. The circuit can be wired to these contacts, with the method of switching as shown in figure 7.3. The output of each 4024 is routed to its appropriate position on the keyboard by 47 kΩ resistors (other values can be used if emphasis is needed at one end of the keyboard). The other ends of these resistors are earthed via a rhodium bar which is threaded through the contacts. In this way the signals from the notes *not* being played pass to chassis and cannot be heard as interference on the output. As a note is played, this switch is operated and the earth connection removed to allow the signal, via the 47 kΩ resistor, to pass to the output **busbar**.

The busbars are wired according to the 2 ft, 4 ft, 8 ft or other footages found on the organ keys, two, three or more sets of contacts being provided on each note on to which the 47 kΩ resistors are soldered. The mechanics of each note are shown, an old piano keyboard being suitable if adapted as shown. The sets of contacts are mounted on the ends of each note.

The AY-1-0212 circuit divides the 1 MHz output by 239, 253, and so on, to produce notes C, B, and so on, to an accuracy of about 1 per cent. The inverters formed from another CMOS circuit 4049 are connected as an oscillator and drive circuit; 4024 circuits are used as the 7 octave dividers — 12 of these are needed, each wired as note C as shown.

The squarewaves sound very uninteresting and harsh so filter circuits are added to each busbar output to create flute, trumpet, string or other musical sound. The filter circuits of chapter 3 are well suited; the organ stops switch these filters to the output mixer and power amplifier (again see chapters 3 and 4).

The CMOS circuits require various supply voltages, −13 V and −26 V; the power supply circuit of figure 5.6c is adapted for these voltages.

Electronic **pianos** use the same basic generator as above, the only difference being in the attack and decay of the piano notes. The circuit of figure 5.4b is used with the 4024 outputs being filtered to produce sinewave signals, then passing to point B of figure 5.4b. The keyboard switches operate the switch of this same attack/decay circuit, one circuit and filter being necessary for every note of the piano. The attack and decay adjustments can be fixed, the outputs all being paralleled up via 47 kΩ resistors in a gigantic mixer amplifier. A small 2-octave piano is not too complex and should be within your capabilities. Modern ICs are now available to provide this **keying** of the piano, but this is beyond the scope of this book.

7.3 Fun Circuits

Here are three final circuits using the BC107/8 and BC177 transistors to generate strange sounds (figure 7.4). I won't describe the sound of the circuit in figure 7.4a except to say that it makes a nice toy for a child. The circuit in figure 7.4b delivers a wailing **siren** sound as switch S closes and opens, and the circuit in figure 7.4c produces a similar **fuzz** noise to the 741 circuit described earlier.

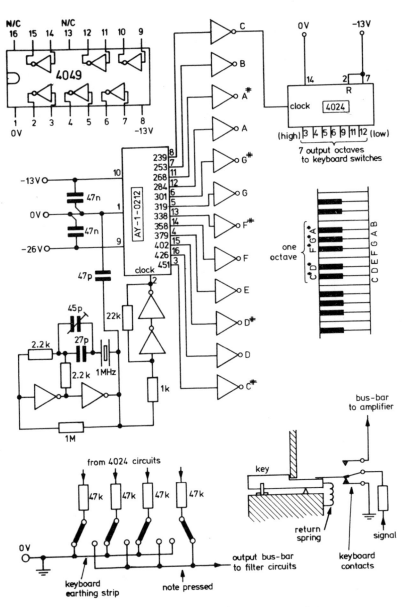

Figure 7.3   Electronic organ generator

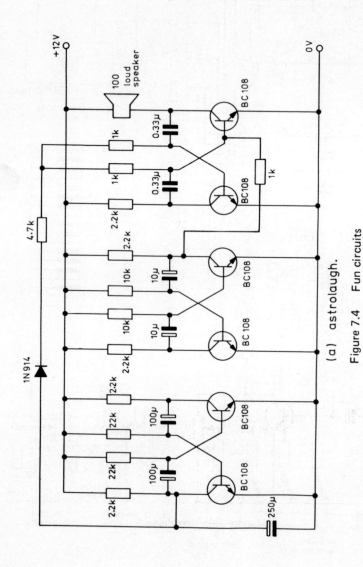

(a) astrolaugh.

Figure 7.4   Fun circuits

(b)
siren

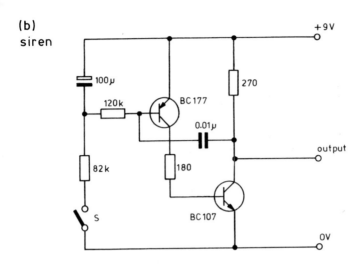

(c)
fuzz box

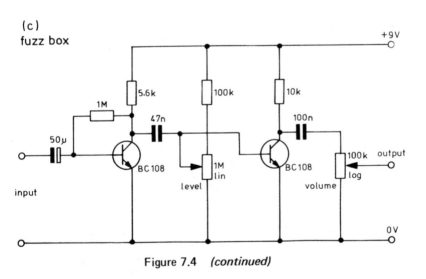

Figure 7.4   *(continued)*

Appendix I

Section 1.1.1 referred to decibel gain and the advantages of using decibels rather than voltage and current ratios, because decibels can be added and subtracted rather than multiplied and divided thus greatly simplifying the mathematics. For example, an amplifier with a gain of 60 dB which is preceded by an attenuator of 5 dB loss and followed by output leads of 3 dB loss has an over-all gain of $60 - 5 - 3 = 52$ dB. Voltage, current or power gain can be converted into decibel gain using one of the following formulae

$$\text{dB voltage gain} = 20 \log_{10} \frac{V_{out}}{V_{in}} \tag{1}$$

$$\text{dB current gain} = 20 \log_{10} \frac{I_{out}}{I_{in}} \tag{2}$$

$$\text{dB power gain} = 10 \log_{10} \frac{P_{out}}{P_{in}} \tag{3}$$

Equations 1 and 2 are derived from equation 3 and both assume that the amplifier input and output resistances are equal. This assumption is seldom true and so dB measurements are often misleading. The values of V_{out}, I_{in}, and so on, use r.m.s. values rather than peak-to-peak, the r.m.s. value being indicated on most ac meters. Oscilloscopes indicate the peak-to-peak value; r.m.s. is found from

$$\text{r.m.s.} = \frac{\text{peak-to-peak}}{2\sqrt{2}} \text{ or } \frac{\text{peak value}}{\sqrt{2}} \text{ or peak value} \times 0.707$$

More is said in chapter 1 about specification figures which can be misleading also, like most statistics. The most accurate figure to observe is the dB power gain.

The horizontal scale of a frequency response also uses a logarithmic scale of frequency, with equal spacing between 10, 10^2, 10^3, 10^4, and so on. The reference point is 1 kHz which often sets 0 dB, every other frequency being measured against this, with corresponding dB values. A **negative** dB figure represents a **loss** in gain. Some frequency responses show a vertical scale with 0 dB at the base and +5 dB, +10 dB, and so on, vertically upwards; either form is acceptable.

Table 1.1 shows a few typical conversions between dB values and voltage, current or power gain and section 1.1.3 refers to a further application of decibel measurement concerning **sound intensities**. Sound intensities are measured as power levels ($\mu W/m^2$) on a measuring instrument; the values are listed in table 1.2. In order that these power levels might be meaningful, they are all related to the **threshold of hearing** which is referred to as a power level of 10^{-6} W/m^2 or 0 dB. Each dB value is then calculated using equation (3). For example, heavy traffic corresponds to 10 $\mu W/m^2$, so

$$\text{dB sound level} = 10 \log_{10} \frac{\text{sound intensity}}{\text{threshold level}}$$

$$= 10 \log_{10} \frac{10}{10^{-6}}$$

$$= 10 \log_{10} 10^7$$

$$= 10 \times 7$$

$$= 70 \text{ dB}$$

Appendix II Components required for Projects

Single Transistor Amplifiers — Low Impedance Input
(Figure 3.1a)

Resistors	470 Ω	$\frac{1}{8}$ W
	1 kΩ	$\frac{1}{8}$ W
	6.8 kΩ	$\frac{1}{8}$ W
	18 kΩ	$\frac{1}{8}$ W
Capacitors	10 μF	10 V electrolytic
	25 μF	10 V electrolytic
Semiconductors	any *pnp* germanium transistor e.g. OC71 series	

Treble Booster Amplifier (Figure 3.1b)

Resistors	10 kΩ	$\frac{1}{8}$ W
	1.5 MΩ	$\frac{1}{8}$ W
	1 kΩ	lin. variable preset
Capacitors		
	10 μF	10 V electrolytic (two)
Semiconductors	BC108	

Sundries	primary winding of any mains or output transformer (high Z side)

Loud Hailer (Figure 3.1c)

Resistors	33 Ω	$\frac{1}{2}$ W
	470 Ω	$\frac{1}{2}$ W
Capacitors	47 μF	16 V electrolytic
Semiconductors	2N3055 on suitable heat sink (see text)	
Sundries	carbon insert microphone	

Preamplifier Circuits (Figure 3.2a)

Resistors	5.6 kΩ	$\frac{1}{8}$ W
	330 kΩ	$\frac{1}{8}$ W
Capacitors	8 μF	16 V electrolytic
	16 μF	16 V electrolytic
Semiconductors	BC108	

(Figure 3.2b)

Resistors	2.2 kΩ	$\frac{1}{8}$ W
	4.7 kΩ	$\frac{1}{8}$ W (two)
	560 kΩ	$\frac{1}{8}$ W
Capacitors	16 μF	16 V electrolytic
	50 μF	16 V electrolytic (two)
Semiconductors	BC108, BC177	

(Figure 3.2c)

Resistors	4.7 kΩ	$\frac{1}{8}$ W (two)
	6.8 kΩ	$\frac{1}{8}$ W
	270 kΩ	$\frac{1}{8}$ W
Capacitors	8 μF	16 V electrolytic
	16 μF	16 V electrolytic
	50 μF	16 V electrolytic
Semiconductors	BC108 (two)	

(Figure 3.2d)

Resistors		
	$3.3\,k\Omega$	$\frac{1}{8}$ W
	$82\,k\Omega$	$\frac{1}{8}$ W
	$100\,k\Omega$	$\frac{1}{8}$ W
	$180\,k\Omega$	$\frac{1}{8}$ W
	$120\,k\Omega$	$\frac{1}{8}$ W

Capacitors		
	$3\,\mu F$	(C_F) 16 V electrolytic
	$1\,\mu F$	16 V electrolytic
	$16\,\mu F$	16 V electrolytic

Semiconductors   BC108 (two)

(Figure 3.2e)

Resistors		
	$100\,\Omega$	$\frac{1}{8}$ W
	$470\,\Omega$	$\frac{1}{8}$ W
	$820\,\Omega$	$\frac{1}{8}$ W
	$1\,k\Omega$	$\frac{1}{8}$ W
	$10\,k\Omega$	$\frac{1}{8}$ W
	$12\,k\Omega$	$\frac{1}{8}$ W
	$47\,k\Omega$	$\frac{1}{8}$ W
	$100\,k\Omega$	$\frac{1}{8}$ W

Capacitors		
	$2\,\mu F$	16 V electrolytic (two)
	470 nF	16 V polyester

Semiconductors   BC108

(Figure 3.2f)

Resistors		
	$10\,k\Omega$	$\frac{1}{8}$ W
	$100\,k\Omega$	$\frac{1}{8}$ W (two)
	$2.2\,k\Omega$	$\frac{1}{8}$ W preset

Capacitors		
	$1.5\,\mu F$	16 V electrolytic
	$2\,\mu F$	16 V electrolytic
	$47\,\mu F$	16 V electrolytic

Semiconductors   BC108 (two)

General Purpose Preamplifier (Figure 3.3a)

Resistors	470 Ω	$\frac{1}{8}$ W
	680 Ω	$\frac{1}{8}$ W
	1 kΩ	$\frac{1}{8}$ W
	2.2 kΩ	$\frac{1}{8}$ W
	5.6 kΩ	$\frac{1}{8}$ W
	15 kΩ	$\frac{1}{8}$ W
	180 kΩ	$\frac{1}{8}$ W
	100 kΩ	lin. potentiometer (volume)

Capacitors	100 pF	mica or ceramic
	18 pF	mica or ceramic
	0.47 F	ceramic or polyester
	2 F	16 V electrolytic
	6.8 F	16 V electrolytic
	10 F	16 V electrolytic
	68 F	16 V electrolytic

Semiconductors	BC108 (two)

AGC Controlled Amplifier (Figure 3.3b)

Resistors	1 kΩ	$\frac{1}{8}$ W
	2.2 kΩ	$\frac{1}{8}$ W (two)
	680 Ω	$\frac{1}{8}$ W
	15 kΩ	$\frac{1}{8}$ W
	27 kΩ	$\frac{1}{8}$ W
	100 kΩ	$\frac{1}{8}$ W
	10 kΩ	$\frac{1}{8}$ W

Capacitors	10 F	16 V electrolytic
	47 F	16 V electrolytic (three)

Semiconductors	BC108 (three), 1N914 (two)

Switched Preamplifier (Figure 3.4)

Resistors		
470 Ω	$\frac{1}{8}$ W	
1 kΩ	$\frac{1}{8}$ W	
1.2 kΩ	$\frac{1}{8}$ W	
1.8 kΩ	$\frac{1}{8}$ W	
47 Ω	$\frac{1}{8}$ W	
3.3 kΩ	$\frac{1}{8}$ W	
6.2 kΩ	$\frac{1}{8}$ W	
12 kΩ	$\frac{1}{8}$ W	
22 kΩ	$\frac{1}{8}$ W	
47 kΩ	$\frac{1}{8}$ W	
2.2 kΩ	$\frac{1}{8}$ W	
56 kΩ	$\frac{1}{8}$ W	
82 kΩ	$\frac{1}{8}$ W	
100 kΩ	$\frac{1}{8}$ W	
220 kΩ	$\frac{1}{8}$ W (two)	
820 kΩ	$\frac{1}{8}$ W (two)	

Capacitors		
4.7 pF	ceramic
18 pF	ceramic
1.5 nF	ceramic
2.2 nF	ceramic
4.7 nF	ceramic
1 μF	40 V electrolytic
6.8 μF	40 V electrolytic (two)
10 μF	40 V electrolytic

Semiconductors   BC108 (three)

Sundries   two-pole   three-way switch

Microphone Preamplifier (Figure 3.5)

Resistors		
470 Ω	$\frac{1}{8}$ W
3.3 kΩ	$\frac{1}{8}$ W
15 kΩ	$\frac{1}{8}$ W
22 kΩ	$\frac{1}{8}$ W
100 kΩ	$\frac{1}{8}$ W
5 kΩ	preset

Capacitors	10 pF	ceramic
	1 μF	40 V electrolytic
	6.8 μF	40 V electrolytic
	47 μF	40 V electrolytic
	100 μF	40 V electrolytic
	470 μF	40 V electrolytic

Semiconductors	2N3819, BC108 (two), 6.8 V Zener 400 mW or smaller

Sundries	balanced input microphone transformer

Hybrid Preamplifier (Figure 3.6)

Resistors	10 kΩ	$\frac{1}{8}$ W
	22 kΩ	$\frac{1}{8}$ W
	5 kΩ	lin. control
	100 kΩ	log control
	100 kΩ	lin. control (two)

Capacitors	8200 pF	ceramic

Semiconductors	HY5 preamplifier

Sundries	two-pole, five-way switch, on/off switch, ±30 V supply

RIAA Magnetic Cartridge Amplifier (Figure 3.7)

Resistors	240 Ω	$\frac{1}{8}$ W
	2.2 kΩ	$\frac{1}{8}$ W
	47 kΩ	$\frac{1}{8}$ W
	100 kΩ	$\frac{1}{8}$ W (two)
	1.2 MΩ	$\frac{1}{8}$ W

Capacitors	1 nF	ceramic
	3.3 nF	ceramic
	100 nF	ceramic
	20 μF	40 V electrolytic

Semiconductors	LM381

741 Circuits (Figure 3.8a)

Resistors	1 kΩ	$\frac{1}{8}$ W
	100 kΩ	$\frac{1}{8}$ W
Capacitors	10 μF	25 V electrolytic
Semiconductors	741	

(Figure 3.8b)

Resistors	47 kΩ	$\frac{1}{8}$ W (two)
Capacitors	0.1 μF	ceramic
	1 μF	25 V electrolytic non-polarised
Semiconductors	741	

(Figure 3.8c)

Resistors	10 kΩ	$\frac{1}{8}$ W (two)
	22 kΩ	log
	100 kΩ	log
Capacitors	10 nF	ceramic (two)
	47 nF	ceramic (two)
Semiconductors	741	

(Figure 3.8d)

Resistors	10 kΩ	$\frac{1}{8}$ W
	82 kΩ	$\frac{1}{8}$ W
	91 kΩ	$\frac{1}{8}$ W
Capacitors	1 μF	25 V electrolytic
	20 μF	25 V electrolytic
Semiconductors	741	

(Figure 3.8e)

Resistors	100 Ω	$\frac{1}{8}$ W (two)
	910 Ω	$\frac{1}{8}$ W
	10 kΩ	$\frac{1}{8}$ W
	47 kΩ	$\frac{1}{8}$ W
	100 kΩ	$\frac{1}{8}$ W
	2.2 MΩ	$\frac{1}{8}$ W

Capacitors	470 nF	ceramic (two)
Semiconductors	741, BC108	

(Figure 3.8f)

Resistors	10 kΩ	$\frac{1}{8}$ W (three)
	47 kΩ	$\frac{1}{8}$ W
	100 kΩ	$\frac{1}{8}$ W
	4.7 kΩ	lin.
	10 kΩ	lin.

Capacitors	15 nF	ceramic
Semiconductors	741 (two)	

(Figure 3.8g)

Resistors	10 kΩ	$\frac{1}{8}$ W
	10 MΩ	$\frac{1}{8}$ W
	100 kΩ	$\frac{1}{8}$ W
	5 kΩ	lin.
	500 kΩ	log

Capacitors	6.8 nF	ceramic
	100 nF	ceramic
Semiconductors	741	

Mixer Amplifiers (Figure 3.9)

Resistors	27 kΩ	$\frac{1}{8}$ W
	33 kΩ	$\frac{1}{8}$ W
	220 kΩ	$\frac{1}{8}$ W
	500 kΩ	lin. per channel

Capacitors	100 nF	ceramic
	1 μF	40 V electrolytic
Semiconductors	LM381 or 741	

Audio Mixer (Figure 3.10)

Resistors		
	47 kΩ	$\frac{1}{8}$ W(five)
	100 kΩ	$\frac{1}{8}$ W
	25 kΩ	lin. (three)

Capacitors		
	0.47 µF	polyester (three)
	10 µF	16 V electrolytic
	25 µF	16 V electrolytic

Semiconductors	741

Scratch/Rumble Filters (Figure 3.11)

Resistors		
	3.9 kΩ	$\frac{1}{8}$ W
	68 kΩ	$\frac{1}{8}$ W
	100 kΩ	$\frac{1}{8}$ W
	820 kΩ	$\frac{1}{8}$ W

Capacitors		
	1 nF	ceramic
	3.9 nF	ceramic
	5.6 nF	ceramic
	68 nF	ceramic (three)

Semiconductors	741 (two)

Simple Tone Control (Figure 3.12)

Resistors		
	270 Ω	$\frac{1}{8}$ W
	1.8 kΩ	$\frac{1}{8}$ W (two)
	3.3 kΩ	$\frac{1}{8}$ W (two)
	10 kΩ	$\frac{1}{8}$ W (four)
	330 kΩ	$\frac{1}{8}$ W
	680 kΩ	$\frac{1}{8}$ W
	100 kΩ	lin. (two)
	500 kΩ	lin.

Capacitors		
	100 pF	ceramic
	1 nF	ceramic
	4.7 nF	ceramic
	5.6 nF	ceramic

22 nF	ceramic
0.47 μF	polyester
4.7 μF	16 V electrolytic
22 μF	16 V electrolytic

Semiconductors   741 (two)

Passive Tone Control (Figure 3.13)

Resistors		
	560 Ω	$\frac{1}{8}$ W
	5.6 kΩ	$\frac{1}{8}$ W
	8.2 kΩ	$\frac{1}{8}$ W
	10 kΩ	$\frac{1}{8}$ W
	82 kΩ	$\frac{1}{8}$ W
	50 kΩ	log (three)
	100 kΩ	lin.

Capacitors		
	2.2 nF	ceramic
	22 nF	ceramic
	47 nF	ceramic
	470 nF	polyester
	1 μF	10 V electrolytic

Tone Control (Figure 3.14)

Resistors		
	2.2 kΩ	$\frac{1}{8}$ W
	3.3 kΩ	$\frac{1}{8}$ W (two)
	10 kΩ	$\frac{1}{8}$ W
	47 kΩ	$\frac{1}{8}$ W (two)
	100 kΩ	$\frac{1}{8}$ W
	220 kΩ	$\frac{1}{8}$ W
	330 kΩ	$\frac{1}{8}$ W
	500 kΩ	lin.
	100 kΩ	lin.

Capacitors		
	10 pF	silver mica
	6.8 nF	ceramic (two)
	1.5 nF	
	2.2 μF	40 V electrolytic (two)
	10 μF	40 V electrolytic
	22 μF	40 V electrolytic

Semiconductors   BC107 (two)

Electronic Attenuator (Figure 3.15)

Resistors	4–33 kΩ lin.	
Capacitors	620 pF	ceramic
	1 μF	16 V electrolytic
	47 μF	16 V electrolytic
Semiconductors	MC3340P	

Electronic Tone Control (Figure 3.16)

Resistors	82 kΩ	$\frac{1}{8}$ W (three)
	25 kΩ	lin. (three)
Capacitors	200 pF	ceramic (two)
	1 nF	ceramic
	0.22 μF	polyester
	1 μF	16 V electrolytic
	47 μF	16 V electrolytic
Semiconductors	MC3340P (three)	

1 W Amplifier (Figure 4.1)

Resistors	3.9 Ω	$\frac{1}{8}$ W (two)
	4.7 Ω	$\frac{1}{2}$ W (two)
	2.2 kΩ	$\frac{1}{8}$ W (two)
	10 kΩ	$\frac{1}{8}$ W
	180 kΩ	$\frac{1}{8}$ W (two)
Capacitors	1 μF	16 V electrolytic
Semiconductors	741, 2N3300 or BD131, 2N3134 or BD132, 1N4148 (two)	
Sundries	15 Ω speaker	

Intercom (Figure 4.2)

Resistors		
	2.2 kΩ	$\frac{1}{8}$ W
	4.7 kΩ	$\frac{1}{8}$ W (two)
	10 kΩ	$\frac{1}{8}$ W
	47 kΩ	$\frac{1}{8}$ W
	100 kΩ	$\frac{1}{8}$ W

Capacitors		
	0.01 μF	ceramic
	4.7 μF	16 V electrolytic
	10 μF	16 V electrolytic (three)

Semiconductors   BC108 (two), 2N3053

Sundries   35 Ω speaker (two), two-pole changeover switch

10 W Amplifier (Figure 4.3)

Resistors		
	0.47 Ω	$\frac{1}{2}$ W (two)
	10 Ω	$\frac{1}{8}$ W (two)
	22 Ω	$\frac{1}{8}$ W
	100 Ω	$\frac{1}{8}$ W
	270 Ω	$\frac{1}{8}$ W (two)
	10 kΩ	$\frac{1}{8}$ W
	100 kΩ	$\frac{1}{8}$ W
	100 Ω	preset

Capacitors		
	1 nF	ceramic
	47 nF	ceramic
	0.01 μF	ceramic
	0.22 μF	polyester
	15 μF	40 V electrolytic
	22 μF	40 V electrolytic
	150 μF	40 V electrolytic
	470 μF	40 V electrolytic
	2200 μF	40 V electrolytic

Semiconductors   BC158, BC108, BD131, BD132

Sundries   8 Ω speaker

2 W Amplifier (Figure 4.4)

Resistors	68 kΩ	$\frac{1}{8}$ W
	10 kΩ	lin.
	25 kΩ	lin.
Capacitors	0.047 μF	ceramic
	470 μF	16 V electrolytic
Semiconductors	LM380	
Sundries	8 Ω speaker, heat sink	

LM380 Amplifier (Figure 4.5)

Resistors	2.7 Ω	$\frac{1}{8}$ W
	2 MΩ	log
Capacitors	0.1 μF	polyester
	470 μF	6.3 V electrolytic
Semiconductors	LM380	
Sundries	8 Ω speaker, heat sink	

Stereo 2 + 2 Amplifier (Figure 4.6a)

Resistors	2.2 kΩ	$\frac{1}{8}$ W (two)
	100 kΩ	$\frac{1}{8}$ W (two)
	1 MΩ	$\frac{1}{8}$ W (two)
Capacitors	5 nF	ceramic (two)
	5 μF	16 V electrolytic (two)
	220 μF	16 V electrolytic (two)
	250 μF	16 V electrolytic
Semiconductors	LM377	
Sundries	8 Ω speaker (two)	

VU Meter (Figure 4.6b)

Resistors	100 kΩ	preset (two)
	6.8 kΩ	$\frac{1}{8}$ W (two)
Capacitors	4.7 μF	6.3 V electrolytic (two)
Semiconductors	OA47 (eight)	
Sundries	circuit for figure 4.6a, VU meter 200 μA (two)	

4 W Amplifier (Figure 4.7)

Resistors	1 Ω	$\frac{1}{8}$ W
	2.2 Ω	$\frac{1}{8}$ W
	220 Ω	$\frac{1}{8}$ W
Capacitors	100 nF	ceramic
	2.2 μF	16 V electrolytic
	100 μF	16 V electrolytic
	470 μF	16 V electrolytic
	1000 μF	16 V electrolytic
Semiconductors	TDA2002(A)	
Sundries	2 Ω speaker	

16 W Amplifier (Figure 4.7)

Resistors	10 kΩ	$\frac{1}{8}$ W
	100 kΩ	$\frac{1}{8}$ W
	1 MΩ	$\frac{1}{8}$ W
Capacitors	0.1 μF	polyester
	0.47 μF	polyester
	250 μF	16 V electrolytic
Semiconductors	LM379	
Sundries	16 Ω speaker	

21 W Amplifier (Figure 4.8)

Resistors		
	1 Ω	$\frac{1}{8}$ W
	3.3 kΩ	$\frac{1}{8}$ W
	100 kΩ	$\frac{1}{8}$ W (two)
	and 100 kΩ	$\frac{1}{8}$ W (three for single supply)

Capacitors		
	100 nF	ceramic (three)
	1 μF	16 V electrolytic
	4.7 μF	16 V electrolytic

Semiconductors	TDA2030

Sundries	4–8 Ω speaker

25 W Amplifier (Figure 4.9)

Resistors	22 Ω	$\frac{1}{4}$ W

Capacitors	0.1 μF	polyester

Semiconductors	HY50

Sundries	4–16 Ω speaker, 1.5 A fuse

20 W Amplifier (Figure 4.10)

Resistors		
	0.5 Ω	$\frac{1}{2}$ W (two)
	10 Ω	$\frac{1}{8}$ W
	22 Ω	$\frac{1}{8}$ W (two)
	100 Ω	$\frac{1}{8}$ W
	150 Ω	$\frac{1}{8}$ W (two)
	220 Ω	$\frac{1}{8}$ W (two)
	470 Ω	$\frac{1}{8}$ W
	680 Ω	$\frac{1}{8}$ W
	4.1 kΩ	$\frac{1}{8}$ W (two)
	82 kΩ	$\frac{1}{8}$ W
	10 kΩ	log
	470 Ω	preset

Capacitors		
	69 pF	ceramic
	0.1 μF	polyester
	1 μF	40 V electrolytic
	100 μF	16 V electrolytic

Semiconductors	741, BC182 (two), BC212, 2N3055 (*pnp*), 2N3055 (*npn*)
Sundries	8 Ω speaker

9/20/40/70 W Amplifier (Figure 4.11)

Resistors	0.22 Ω	$\frac{1}{8}$ W or 0.1 Ω $\frac{1}{8}$ W
	33 Ω	$\frac{1}{8}$ W (three)
	470 Ω	$\frac{1}{8}$ W
	1 kΩ	$\frac{1}{8}$ W (three)
	4.7 kΩ	$\frac{1}{8}$ W (two)
	47 kΩ	$\frac{1}{8}$ W
	56 kΩ	$\frac{1}{8}$ W
	100 kΩ	$\frac{1}{8}$ W

Capacitors	100 pF	ceramic
	820 pF	ceramic
	10 nF	ceramic
	47 nF	ceramic (two)
	2 μF	40 V electrolytic
	10 μF	40 V electrolytic
	100 μF	40 V electrolytic
	220 μF	35 V electrolytic

Semiconductors	BC107 (two), BC177 (two), BFY51 (two), 2N3055 (two), 1N914 (two)
Sundries	speaker

50 W Amplifier (Figure 4.12)

Resistors	1 Ω	1 W
	10 Ω	1 W
	0.15 Ω	$\frac{1}{2}$ W (two)
	100 Ω	$\frac{1}{8}$ W (two)
	1 kΩ	$\frac{1}{8}$ W (five)
	4.7 kΩ	$\frac{1}{8}$ W (two)
	47 kΩ	$\frac{1}{8}$ W
	100 kΩ	$\frac{1}{8}$ W (three)
	10 kΩ	preset

Capacitors	4.7 pF	silver mica (two)
	1 nF	ceramic (three)
	47 nF	ceramic
	100 nF	ceramic (four)
	1 μF	40 V electrolytic
	4.7 μF	25 V electrolytic
	10 μF	40 V electrolytic (two)

| Semiconductors | LM391, BD139, BD140, 2N3055 (*pnp*), 2N3055 (*npn*), 1N4002 (two) |

| Sundries | 8 Ω speaker, 6 μH inductor (see text) |

100 W Amplifier (Figure 4.13)

| Resistors | none |

| Capacitors | 4700 μF   40 V electrolytic (four) |

| Semiconductors | B40, C500 (four) |

| Sundries | 240 V: 25 + 25 V 4A transformer, 1.25 A fuse and holder, 6.3 A fuse and holder (two) |

Active Cross-over (Figure 4.15)

Resistors	1 Ω	$\frac{1}{8}$ W
	1 kΩ	$\frac{1}{8}$ W (five)
	1.8 kΩ	$\frac{1}{8}$ W
	2.2 kΩ	$\frac{1}{8}$ W
	3.3 kΩ	$\frac{1}{8}$ W
	4.7 kΩ	$\frac{1}{8}$ W
	6.8 kΩ	$\frac{1}{8}$ W (three)
	22 kΩ	$\frac{1}{8}$ W (two)
	56 kΩ	$\frac{1}{8}$ W
	100 kΩ	$\frac{1}{8}$ W (two)
	220 kΩ	$\frac{1}{8}$ W
	5 kΩ	lin. (two)
	1 kΩ	lin.

Capacitors	6.8 nF	ceramic
	100 nF	ceramic
	180 nF	ceramic
	330 nF	ceramic
	470 nF	ceramic (two)

Semiconductors	BC108 (four)

Sundries	power amplifier (two)

Power Supply (Fixed) (Figure 4.18a)

Resistors	1 kΩ	$\frac{1}{8}$ W
	2.2 kΩ	$\frac{1}{8}$ W
	10 kΩ	$\frac{1}{8}$ W (two)
	5 kΩ	lin.

Capacitors	none

Semiconductors	741, BFY51, 6.2 V Zener 400 mW

Power Supply (Variable) (Figure 4.18b)

Resistors	120 Ω	$\frac{1}{8}$ W
	270 Ω	$\frac{1}{8}$ W
	2.7 kΩ	$\frac{1}{8}$ W
	20 kΩ	lin.

Capacitors	none

Semiconductors	741, AD161, 18 V Zener 400 mW

2 A Supply (Figure 4.19a)

Resistors	270 Ω	$\frac{1}{8}$ W or 680 Ω $\frac{1}{8}$ W

Capacitors	100 μF	25 V electrolytic
	2200 μF	25 V electrolytic

Semiconductors	1N5408 (four), BC107, 2N3055, 13 V or 18 V Zener 400 mW

Sundries	240 V : 12 or 17 V transformer 2 A

5 A Supply (Figure 4.19b)

Resistors	680 Ω	$\frac{1}{8}$ W or 1 kΩ $\frac{1}{8}$ W
	100 Ω	$\frac{1}{8}$ W
	1.8 kΩ	$\frac{1}{8}$ W
	10 kΩ	$\frac{1}{8}$ W (two)

Capacitors	2200, 4700 or 10 000 μF electrolytic (see text)
	47 nF ceramic
	47 μF 50 V electrolytic

Semiconductors	four diodes (see text), 33 or 43 V Zener 1 W, BFY51 (three), 2N3055

Sundries	240 V : 30 or 42 V transformer (see text)

Attack/Decay Circuit (Figure 5.2)

Resistors	4.7 kΩ	$\frac{1}{8}$ W (two)
	10 kΩ	$\frac{1}{8}$ W
	39 kΩ	$\frac{1}{8}$ W
	47 kΩ	$\frac{1}{8}$ W
	680 kΩ	$\frac{1}{8}$ W (two)
	100 kΩ	lin.
	680 kΩ	lin.

Capacitors	39 nF	ceramic (two)
	100 nF	ceramic (two)
	10 μF	16 V electrolytic

Semiconductors	BC108 (five)

Sundries	on/off switch

Rhythm Beat Generator (Figure 5.3a)

Resistors	12 kΩ	$\frac{1}{8}$ W (two)
	27 kΩ	$\frac{1}{8}$ W
	120 kΩ	$\frac{1}{8}$ W

Capacitors	2 μF	16 V electrolytic (two)

Semiconductors	any *pnp* low power transistors

Rhythm Drum Voicer (Figure 5.3b)

Resistors	2.2 kΩ	$\frac{1}{8}$ W
	15 kΩ	$\frac{1}{8}$ W
	22 kΩ	$\frac{1}{8}$ W (two)
	68 kΩ	$\frac{1}{8}$ W (two)
	150 kΩ	$\frac{1}{8}$ W
	390 kΩ	$\frac{1}{8}$ W

Capacitors	2.2 nF	ceramic (three)
	500 pF	ceramic
	0.1 μF	polyester

Semiconductors	BC108

Brush/Cymbals Circuit (Figure 5.3c)

Resistors	680 Ω	$\frac{1}{8}$ W
	2.2 kΩ	$\frac{1}{8}$ W
	10 kΩ	$\frac{1}{8}$ W (two)
	68 kΩ	$\frac{1}{8}$ W (two)
	100 kΩ	$\frac{1}{8}$ W (two)
	150 kΩ	$\frac{1}{8}$ W
	1.2 MΩ	$\frac{1}{8}$ W
	10 kΩ	lin.
	500 kΩ	lin.

Capacitors	6.8 nF	ceramic
	0.1 μF	polyester
	0.22 μF	polyester
	0.02 μF	ceramic
	2 μF	16 V electrolytic
	4 μF	16 V electrolytic
	10 μF	16 V electrolytic

Semiconductors	BC108, OA81, noisy Zener

Synthesiser Modulator (Figure 5.4a)

Resistors		
220 Ω	$\frac{1}{8}$ W	
470 Ω	$\frac{1}{8}$ W (three)	
1 kΩ	$\frac{1}{8}$ W (three)	
4.7 kΩ	$\frac{1}{8}$ W (two)	
10 kΩ	$\frac{1}{8}$ W	
15 kΩ	$\frac{1}{8}$ W	
33 kΩ	$\frac{1}{8}$ W (two)	
47 kΩ	$\frac{1}{8}$ W	
1 MΩ	$\frac{1}{8}$ W	
10 kΩ	lin.	

Capacitors		
0.22 μF	polyester
1 μF	16 V electrolytic
2 μF	16 V electrolytic
8 μF	16 V electrolytic
10 μF	16 V electrolytic
16 μF	16 V electrolytic
100 μF	16 V electrolytic (two)

Semiconductors   BC108 (three), MPF105

Envelope Shaper (Figure 5.4b)

Resistors		
56 Ω	$\frac{1}{8}$ W
470 Ω	$\frac{1}{8}$ W
1 kΩ	$\frac{1}{8}$ W
2.2 kΩ	$\frac{1}{8}$ W (two)
20 kΩ	lin.
100 kΩ	lin. (two)
1 MΩ	lin.
2 MΩ	lin.

Capacitors		
1 μF	16 V electrolytic
10 μF	16 V electrolytic (two)

Semiconductors   2N2646, BC108

Sundries   change-over switch (two)

Sound-operated Fader (Figure 5.4d)

Resistors	100 Ω	$\frac{1}{8}$ W
	10 kΩ	$\frac{1}{8}$ W (two)
	22 kΩ	$\frac{1}{8}$ W
Capacitors	0.1 μF	polyester
	100 μF	16 V electrolytic
Semiconductors	BC108, 1N914	
Sundries	circuit of figure 5.4a, mixer circuit of figure 3.10	

IC Rhythm Generator (Figure 5.5)

Resistors	270 Ω	$\frac{1}{8}$ W
	3.9 kΩ	$\frac{1}{8}$ W
	10 kΩ	$\frac{1}{8}$ W
	22 kΩ	$\frac{1}{8}$ W (six)
	100 kΩ	$\frac{1}{8}$ W
	220 kΩ	$\frac{1}{8}$ W
	2.2 MΩ	$\frac{1}{8}$ W
	1 MΩ	log
Capacitors	10 nF	ceramic
	47 nF	ceramic
	220 nF	ceramic
Semiconductors	BC108, LED, 1N4148, M252AA IC, CD4011 (two)	

Rhythm Drum Voicing (Figure 5.6a)

Resistors	10 kΩ	$\frac{1}{8}$ W
	15 kΩ	$\frac{1}{8}$ W
	56 kΩ	$\frac{1}{8}$ W
	68 kΩ	$\frac{1}{8}$ W (two)
	100 kΩ	$\frac{1}{8}$ W
	330 kΩ	$\frac{1}{8}$ W
	470 kΩ	$\frac{1}{8}$ W
	1 MΩ	$\frac{1}{8}$ W
	25 kΩ	preset

Capacitors	15 nF	ceramic (two) } see table on figure
	33 nF	ceramic (two) } 5.13 for alternatives
	50 nF	ceramic
	0.1 μF	polyester

Semiconductors	BC108, 1N914

Rhythm Percussion (Figure 5.6b)

Resistors	2.2 kΩ	$\frac{1}{8}$ W
	4.7 kΩ	$\frac{1}{8}$ W (two)
	10 kΩ	$\frac{1}{8}$ (three)
	22 kΩ	$\frac{1}{8}$ W
	56 kΩ	$\frac{1}{8}$ W
	100 kΩ	$\frac{1}{8}$ W
	390 kΩ	$\frac{1}{8}$ W
	470 kΩ	$\frac{1}{8}$ W
	1 MΩ	$\frac{1}{8}$ W (three)
	220 kΩ	lin. preset
	10 kΩ	preset

Capacitors	4.7 nF	ceramic (two)
	22 nF	ceramic
	47 nF	ceramic
	68 nF	ceramic
	100 nF	polyester (three)
	220 nF	polyester (six)
	330 nF	polyester

Semiconductors	BC108 (four), 741, 1N4148 (three)

Sundries	100 mH inductor (two)

Rhythm Power Supply (Figure 5.6c)

Resistors	4.7 kΩ	$\frac{1}{8}$ W (three)

Capacitors	0.22 μF	polyester (two)
	0.47 μF	polyester (three)
	4700 μF	16 V electrolytic (two)

Semiconductors	7812, 7912, 7805, 1N4002 (four)
Sundries	240 V : 15 + 15 V transformer 0.5 A

Audio Phasing Unit (Figure 5.7)

Resistors	220 Ω	$\frac{1}{8}$ W (two)
	470 Ω	$\frac{1}{8}$ W (two)
	1 kΩ	$\frac{1}{8}$ W (three)
	1.5 kΩ	$\frac{1}{8}$ W (two)
	2.7 kΩ	$\frac{1}{8}$ W
	15 kΩ	$\frac{1}{8}$ W
	47 kΩ	$\frac{1}{8}$ W
	100 kΩ	$\frac{1}{8}$ W (three)
	5 kΩ	lin.
	10 kΩ	lin.
	20 kΩ	preset
	25 kΩ	lin.

Capacitors	0.1 μF	polyester
	6.4 μF	16 V electrolytic (four)
	10 μF	16 V electrolytic (two)
	50 μF	16 V electrolytic

Semiconductors	BC108 (seven), OA47
Sundries	ORP12 (two), 6 V 50 mA lamp (two), on/off switch

Reverberation Unit (Figure 5.8)

Resistors	2.2 kΩ	$\frac{1}{8}$ W
	10 kΩ	$\frac{1}{8}$ W (four)
	120 kΩ	$\frac{1}{8}$ W
	10 kΩ	lin. (two)

Capacitors	1 nF	ceramic
	3 nF	ceramic
	0.1 μF	polyester (two)

Semiconductors	741 (two)
Sundries	1 or 2 W amplifier, spring line unit

Audio Compressor (Figure 5.10a)

Resistors	4.7 Ω	$\frac{1}{8}$ W
	2.2 kΩ	$\frac{1}{8}$ W (two)
	100 kΩ	$\frac{1}{8}$ W (two)
	1 MΩ	lin.
	4.7 kΩ	preset
Capacitors	620 pF	ceramic
	0.47 F	polyester (two)
	10 μF	16 V electrolytic
Semiconductors	2N3819, 741, MC3340P, 1N4148	

Audio Compressor (Figure 5.10b)

Resistors	3.3 kΩ	$\frac{1}{8}$ W
	22 kΩ	$\frac{1}{8}$ W (two)
	330 kΩ	$\frac{1}{8}$ W
	560 kΩ	$\frac{1}{8}$ W
Capacitors	620 pF	ceramic
	0.47 μF	polyester
	1 μF	16 V electrolytic
	4.7 μF	16 V electrolytic
	10 μF	16 V electrolytic (two)
Semiconductors	MC3340, BC108 (two), OA47 (two)	

Peak Overload Detector (Figure 5.11)

Resistors	2.2 kΩ	$\frac{1}{8}$ W
	4.7 kΩ	$\frac{1}{8}$ W
	56 kΩ	$\frac{1}{8}$ W (two)
	100 kΩ	$\frac{1}{8}$ W (two)
	150 kΩ	$\frac{1}{8}$ W
	100 kΩ	preset
Capacitors	0.1 μF	polyester
	0.47 μF	polyester
Semiconductors	LED, 741, 6.2 V Zener 400 mW	

Sound-to-light Modulator (Figure 6.1a)

Resistors	1 kΩ	$\frac{1}{8}$ W
	50 kΩ	lin.
	100 kΩ	lin.

Capacitors	0.5 μF	polyester (mains voltage)
	8 μF	10 V electrolytic

Semiconductors   BC108, BFY51, 1N4004, 3 A 400 V thyristor

Sundries   6 V 50 mA lamp bulb, ORP12

Circuit I of Sound-to-light (One Channel Only) (Figure 6.1b)

Resistors	2.2 kΩ	$\frac{1}{8}$ W
	10 kΩ	$\frac{1}{8}$ W
	22 kΩ	$\frac{1}{8}$ W
	27 kΩ	$\frac{1}{8}$ W
	100 kΩ	$\frac{1}{8}$ W
	220 kΩ	$\frac{1}{8}$ W

Capacitors	0.047 μF	ceramic (mains voltage)
	0.047 μF	ceramic
	0.1 μF	polyester

Semiconductors   1N4148 (two), 1N4004, BRY39 A triac, 3 A 400 V thyristor, LED

Sundries   1 : 1 pulse transformer

Circuit II of Sound-to-light (One required) (Figure 6.1b)

Resistors	470 Ω	$\frac{1}{8}$ W
	10 kΩ	$\frac{1}{8}$ W
	100 kΩ	$\frac{1}{8}$ W
	220 kΩ	$\frac{1}{8}$ W (two)
	270 kΩ	$\frac{1}{8}$ W

Capacitors	0.1 μF	polyester
	470 μF	16 V electrolytic

E.P.3—M

Semiconductors   1N4001 (two), BRY 39 A triac

Sundries   240 V : 12 + 12 V transformer 1 A

Colour Organ (Figure 6.3)

Resistors		
	22 Ω	$\frac{1}{2}$ W
	39 Ω	$\frac{1}{8}$ W (three)
	1 kΩ	$\frac{1}{8}$ W (five)
	10 kΩ	lin. (three)

Capacitors		
	0.022 μF	ceramic
	0.047 μF	ceramic
	0.22 μF	polyester
	50 μF	16 V electrolytic

Semiconductors   BC184 (three), 1N4001 (two), 400 V 8 A triac (three)

Sundries   240 V : 12 + 12 V transformer 1 A, 2 kΩ : 8 kΩ audio coupling transformer (three)

Stylophone (Figure 7.1)

Resistors		
	39 Ω	$\frac{1}{8}$ W
	4.7 kΩ	$\frac{1}{8}$ W
	33 kΩ	$\frac{1}{8}$ W (two)
	1.8 MΩ	$\frac{1}{8}$ W
	2 kΩ	lin. preset
	10 kΩ	lin.
	10 kΩ	preset (eight)

Capacitors		
	3 nF	ceramic
	0.05 μF	ceramic (three)
	0.1 μF	polyester (two)

Semiconductors   BC107, 2N2646

Sundries   stylus, on/off switch

741 Stylophone Oscillator (Figure 7.1b)

Resistors	680 Ω	$\frac{1}{8}$ W
	10 kΩ	$\frac{1}{8}$ W
	22 kΩ	$\frac{1}{8}$ W (nine minimum)
Capacitors	0.047 μF	ceramic
Semiconductors	741	

741 Single Supply (Figure 7.1c)

Resistors	680 Ω	$\frac{1}{8}$ W
	10 kΩ	$\frac{1}{8}$ W
	22 kΩ	$\frac{1}{8}$ W (nine minimum)
	33 kΩ	$\frac{1}{8}$ W (two)
Capacitors	0.047 μF	ceramic
Semiconductors	741	

Electronic Composer (Figure 7.2)

Resistors	47 Ω	$\frac{1}{2}$ W
	470 Ω	$\frac{1}{8}$ W (two)
	1 kΩ	$\frac{1}{8}$ W
	1.2 kΩ	$\frac{1}{8}$ W (two)
	10 kΩ	preset (eight minimum)
Capacitors	56 nF	ceramic
	150 nF	ceramic (two)
	220 nF	ceramic (two)
	470 μF	16 V electrolytic (two)
Semiconductors	BC108 (two)	
	BFY51	
	7495 (two minimum)	
	7400 (two)	
	1N4148 (eight minimum)	
Sundries	switch on/off	
	8 Ω	loudspeaker

Electronic Organ (Figure 7.3)

Resistors		
	1 kΩ	$\frac{1}{8}$ W
	2.2 kΩ	$\frac{1}{8}$ W (two)
	22 kΩ	$\frac{1}{8}$ W
	47 kΩ	(one per output of 4024 divider, approximately 84)

Capacitors		
	27 pF	ceramic or silver mica
	45 pF	trimmer
	47 pF	ceramic or silver mica (three)

Semiconductors   4049 hex-inverter (three)
                    AY-1-0212 MOS-divider
                    4024 divider (twelve)

Sundries   1 MHz   crystal
                    keyboard and contacts/switches (see text)
                        tone circuits and amplifiers

Astrolaugh (Figure 7.4a)

Resistors		
	1 kΩ	$\frac{1}{8}$ W (three)
	2.2 kΩ	$\frac{1}{8}$ W (five)
	4.7 kΩ	$\frac{1}{8}$ W
	10 kΩ	$\frac{1}{8}$ W (two)
	22 kΩ	$\frac{1}{8}$ W (two)

Capacitors		
	0.33 μF	ceramic (two)
	10 μF	16 V electrolytic (two)
	100 μF	16 V electrolytic (two)
	250 μF	16 V electrolytic

Semiconductors   BC108 (six)
                    1N914

Sundries   100 Ω   loudspeaker

Siren (Figure 7.4b)

Resistors	180 Ω	$\frac{1}{8}$ W
	270 Ω	$\frac{1}{8}$ W
	82 kΩ	$\frac{1}{8}$ W
	120 kΩ	$\frac{1}{8}$ W
Capacitors	0.01 μF	ceramic
	100 μF	16 V electrolytic
Semiconductors	BC107	
	BC177	
Sundries	switch on/off	
	amplifier	

Fuzz Box (Figure 7.4c)

Resistors	5.6 kΩ	$\frac{1}{8}$ W
	10 kΩ	$\frac{1}{8}$ W
	100 kΩ	$\frac{1}{8}$ W
	1 MΩ	$\frac{1}{8}$ W
	100 kΩ	log. (volume)
	1 MΩ	lin. (level)
Capacitors	47 nF	ceramic
	100 nF	ceramic
	50 μF	16 V electrolytic
Semiconductors	BC108 (two)	

Appendix III Component Suppliers

Chromasonic Electronics
56 Fortis Green Road
Muswell Hill
London N10 3HN   01-883-3705

Maplin Electronic Supplies
P.O. Box 3
Rayleigh
Essex   0702-715155

Bi-Pak   (for bargain packs of components)
P.O. Box 6
Ware
Herts   0920-61593

HB Electronics
22 Newland Street
Kettering
Northants   0536-83922

Marshall's
40—42 Cricklewood Broadway
London NW2 3ET   01-452-0161

Henry's Radio
404 Edgware Road
London W2 1BN   01-402-8381

Appendix IV Specifications
of Semiconductor Devices

Transistors

	Type	P_{tot}	I_C	V_{ceo}	h_{FE}	f_T	case
AD161	npn Ge	4 W	3 A	20 V	80–320	3 MHz	S055
BC107	npn Si	360 mW	100 mA	45 V	110–450	250 MHz	T018
BC108	npn Si	360 mW	100 mA	20 V	110–800	250 MHz	T018 ⎫ or lockfit
BC109	npn Si	360 mW	100 mA	20 V	200–800	250 MHz	T018 ⎭
BC158	pnp Si	350 mW	−100 mA	−30 V	500(typ)	150 MHz	lockfit
BC177	pnp Si	350 mW	−100 mA	−45 V	500(typ)	250 MHz	T018
BC182	npn Si	300 mW	200 mA	50 V	100–480	150 MHz	T092
BC184	npn Si	300 mW	200 mA	30 V	250(min)	150 MHz	T092 ⎫ or lockfit
BC212	pnp Si	300 mW	−200 mA	−50 V	60–300	200 MHz	T092 ⎭
BD131	npn Si	15 W	3 A	45 V	20(min)	60 MHz	T0126 (med. power)
BD132	pnp Si	15 W	−3 A	−45 V	20(min)	60 MHz	T0126 (med. power)
BD139	npn Si	7.5 W	1.5 A	80 V	40–160	75 MHz	T0126
BD140	pnp Si	7.5 W	−1.5 A	−80 V	40–160	75 MHz	T0126
BFY51	npn Si	800 mW	1 A	30 V	40	50 MHz	T039
2N3053	npn Si	800 mW	1 A	40 V	50–250	100 MHz	T039
2N3055	pnp Si or npn Si	115 W	15 A	60 V	20–70	1 MHz	T03 (high power)
2N3134	pnp Si	600 mW	−600 mA	−35 V	100–300	200 MHz	T05
2N3300	npn Si	800 mW	500 mA	30 V	100–300	250 MHz	T05
2N3819 or MPF105	n-channel FET, with P_{tot} = 200 mW, V_{DG} = 25 V, V_{DS} = 25 V T092 case						
2N2646	unijunction transistor with $V_{B_2} - V_{B_1}$ = 35 V, P_{tot} = 300 mW, I_E = 50 mA						

Diodes

Type		I_f	V_{RRM}	case
0A47	gold-bonded Ge	48 mA	30 V	glass signal diode
0A81 or				
0A91	point-contact Ge	20 mA	100 V	glass signal diode
1N914 or	wiskerless Si	75 mA	100 V	plastic signal diodes
1N4148				(high speed)
1N4001	Si rectifier	1 A	50 V	plastic
1N4002	Si rectifier	1 A	100 V	plastic
1N4003	Si rectifier	1 A	200 V	plastic
1N4004	Si rectifier	1 A	400 V	plastic
1N5408	Si rectifier	3 A	1000 V	high power plastic
B40—C5000	or equiv.	5 A	100 V	high power plastic

Thyristors and triacs

See the text for current and voltage ratings, some common mains (400V) types are:

C103YY 300 mA anode current for 0.2 mA gate current; T092 case
C106 2.5 A anode current for 0.2 mA gate current; case similar to T0126

These above types are very sensitive devices requiring very small gate currents. Other types require higher gate currents although their anode currents are greater:

BTY79 6.4 A anode current for 30 mA gate current; stud-type casing
THY500—40 40 A anode current for 60 mA gate current; stud casing but heat sink essential.
TR1 400—0.35 is a sensitive mains triac requiring 5 mA gate current for 6A output
BT139 is a 115 A triac requiring 35 mA gate current and essential heat sink (plastic)

Triacs require series diacs connected to the gate, the most common being BR100 with breakdown voltage of about 33 V and 2 A peak current.

BRY39A is a programmable unijunction transistor, sometimes called a two-gate thyristor (as in figure 6.1) in a T018 case. It can pass up to 3 A peak current.

Integrated Circuits (see text for pin connections)

LM377 a stereo DIL IC giving 2 W per channel into 8 ohm speakers
LM379 a stereo DIL IC giving 6 W per channel into 8 ohm speakers
LM380 a 2.5 W DIL amplifier which produces a very compact power amplifier
LM381 a stereo low noise preamplifier with 'op. amp' connections
741 a general purpose operational amplifier with 100 dB gain up to 1 MHz
MC334OP an audio electronic 'remote control' attenuator
HY5 and HY50 hybrid preamplifier and power amplifier packages from I.L.P. Electronics
TDA 2002(A) a 4 W stereo amplifier
TDA 2030 a 21 W power amplifier with many protection circuits
M252AA a complete rhythm generator IC using CMOS technology
AY-1-0212 a complete organ divider IC with 1 MHz input, using CMOS technology
7805 1 A regulator IC producing 5 V output
7812 1 A regulator IC producing 12 V output
7912 1 A regulator IC producing −12 V output
7400 TTL quad 2-input NAND gate IC
7495 TTL 4-bit shift register IC
CD4011 CMOS quad 2-input NAND gate IC
CD4024 CMOS 7-stage ripple counter
CD4049 CMOS hex inverter/buffer

Light Dependent Resistor

ORP12 Cadmium sulphide LDR with resistance range 130 Ω (light) to 2.4 kΩ (dark) maximum voltage 110 V and 200 mW

Appendix V Printed Circuit Boards

These printed circuits are available ready made from Maplin Electronic Supplies Ltd, P.O. Box 3, Rayleigh, Essex SS6 8LR.

Tone Control

This board is designed for the circuit shown in figure 3.12.

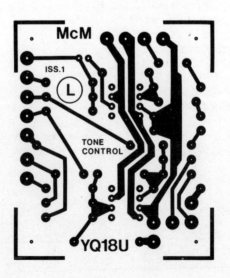

Parts List

R1	330 kΩ
R2	10 kΩ
R3	680 kΩ
R4	1.8 kΩ
R5	3.3 kΩ
R6	10 kΩ
R7	1.8 kΩ
R8	3.3 kΩ
R9	10 kΩ
R10	10 kΩ
R11	270 Ω
C1	0.47 μF
C2	10 nF
C3	22 μF
C4	4.7 nF
C5	5.6 nF
C6	22 nF
C7	56 nF
C8	100 pF
C9	1 nF
C10	4.7 μF
VR1 (treble)	500 kΩ lin.
VR2 (middle)	100 kΩ lin.
VR3 (bass)	100 kΩ lin.
IC1, IC2	741, 8-pin DIL

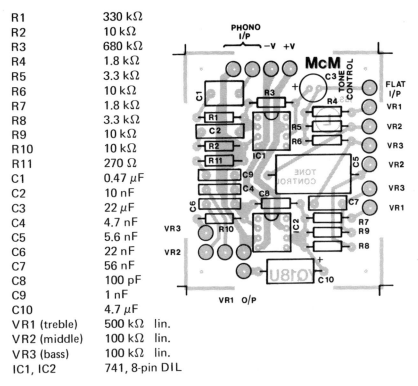

LM380 Amplifiers

This circuit board can be used for either of the two designs in this book. Alternative components are specified below, according to which version is being built.

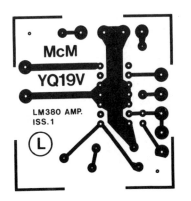

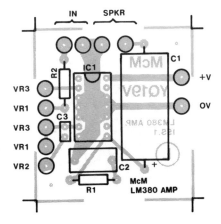

Parts List (figure 4.4a)

R1	wire link
R2	68 kΩ
C1	470 μF
C2	0.047 μF
C3	0.047 μF
VR1	25 kΩ lin.
VR2	10 kΩ lin.
IC1	LM380

(note that the earth connections of VR1 and VR2 are made by a wire link)

Parts List (figure 4.5a)

R1	2.7 Ω
R2	wire link
C1	470 μF
C2	0.1 μF
VR3	2 MΩ log.
IC1	LM380

(note that the upper VR3 connection, which goes to one end of VR3 track and also to the wiper, is linked to the VR1 connection immediately below it)

20 W (2030) Amplifier

This circuit board is designed for the amplifier circuit shown in figure 4.8(a).

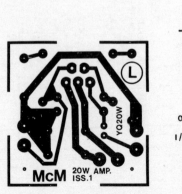

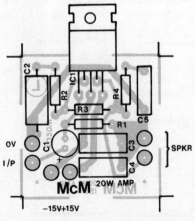

Parts List

R1	100 kΩ	C2	4.7 µF
R2	3.3 kΩ	C3	100 nF
R3	100 kΩ	C4	100 nF
R4	1 Ω	C5	100 nF
C1	1 µF	IC1	TDA2030

Colour Organ

This printed circuit is designed for the Colour Organ design shown in figure 6.3. IMPORTANT: Parts of this board are 'live' to the mains supply in use, so it is vital to take great care with insulation, and in earthing the case if it is fitted in a metal box.

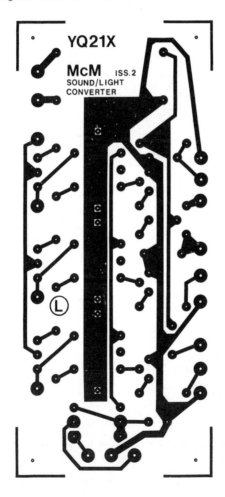

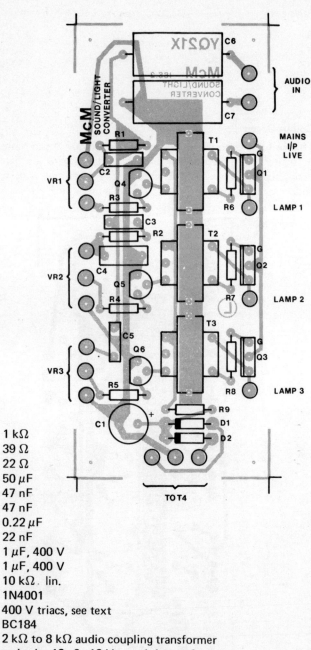

Parts List

R1–R5	1 kΩ
R6, R7, R8	39 Ω
R9	22 Ω
C1	50 μF
C2	47 nF
C3	47 nF
C4	0.22 μF
C5	22 nF
C6	1 μF, 400 V
C7	1 μF, 400 V
VR1–VR3	10 kΩ lin.
D1, D2	1N4001
Q1, Q2, Q3	400 V triacs, see text
Q4, Q5, Q6	BC184
T1, T2, T3	2 kΩ to 8 kΩ audio coupling transformer
T4	mains in, 12–0–12 V out, 1 A transformer